PIONEERS IN MUSIC

The *Goldenen Rebbuhn*
The café where Lanner and Strauss performed

DAVID EWEN

Pioneers

in

Music

Essay Index Reprint Series

BOOKS FOR LIBRARIES PRESS
FREEPORT, NEW YORK

Library of Congress Cataloging in Publication Data

Ewen, David, 1907–
  Pioneers in music.

  (Essay index reprint series)
  Reprinted from the ed. of 1940, New York.
  Bibliography: p.
  1. Composers. 2. Music—History and critic.
3. Music—Discography. I. Title.
ML193.E93P5 1972   780'.92'2   72–6816
ISBN 0-8369-7262-7

CONTENTS

ILLUSTRATIONS

ILLUSTRATIONS

FOREWORD

"*Have the elder races halted?*
Do they droop and end their lesson, weighed over
there beyond the seas?
We take up the task eternal, and the burden,
and the lesson,
Pioneers! O Pioneers!

"*All the past we leave behind*
We debauch upon a newer, mightier world, varied
world,
Fresh and strong the world we seize, world of labor
and the march,
Pioneers! O Pioneers!"

—WALT WHITMAN

THIS is a book about composers great and near-great. Yet it is a book in which such accepted masters as Bach, Handel, Haydn, Mozart, Beethoven, Schubert, Schumann, Brahms, Wagner, and so on, play no major part. Of books about the masters there is an abundance. The layman, therefore, is well informed about these great composers and their achievements. This book, however, hopes to blaze a new trail for the more adventurous lover of music. Here he will find discussed many composers, some of them (like Monteverdi, Gluck and Liszt) with whom he is more or less familiar; but others whom he may not even know by name. But, known or unknown, these are important composers all, and in the development of music they played heroic parts.

This is a book about pioneers in music, those brave adventurers in the world of sound who set out on their own and explored new territories. They are, many of them, the unsung heroes of musical history. Yet how vital has been their work! Haydn, Mozart, and Beethoven are the accepted masters of the piano sonata, symphony, and string quartet. Their work, however, was made possible because others who had preceded them had prepared the materials: stout-hearted and imaginative musicians like Johann Kuhnau of Leipzig, Johann Stamitz of Mannheim, or the members of the early Viennese school. Early composers like Peri, Caccini and—greatest of all—Monteverdi set the stage for the Italian masters of the opera, while Gluck preceded Wagner not only chronologically but aesthetically as well. The concertos of Mozart and Beethoven and Brahms owe their origin to Corelli, who was likewise the father of violin music. And the greatest oratorios of Handel and Bach stem from those of Carissimi, just as the organ works of Bach arose out of those of Buxtehude.

The musical layman, already familiar with the great composers, can gain a more penetrating insight into the subtle evolution of musical form, and a greater understanding of what the masters of music actually accomplished in their own right, if he is first made to recognize the work of music's pioneers. Who these pioneers are, how they first invented the famous forms or (in

[*4*]

other cases) first brought these forms to general acceptance, how they paved the way for the masters is the subject of this book. It is a fascinating subject. It lifts the horizon of music and shows a greater and more varied world than has previously been the experience of the average music lover.

This was not intended to be a history of early music, nor should it be considered as such. No attempt was made either at comprehensiveness or at a coördination of the many varied trends and movements which form the texture of history. Important schools were completely ignored when such schools have not directly influenced either forms of music which are of immediate interest to the concert goer, or those composers with whom he is best acquainted. Many outstanding early composers—some of whom the writer of the book profoundly admires—have also been ignored where discussion of them would have led to a repetition of material.

In writing this book, the author was faced by a major problem. The biographer of Beethoven or Mozart or Brahms has, at least, reasonable assurance that his reader is acquainted with the standard works of the composer under discussion. But this writer was compelled, by the very nature of his subject, to talk about many compositions which he knows are altogether foreign to the reader. Words alone can never convey to a reader the essential qualities of a musical work. Music should be seen or heard before it is read about. The idea of publishing musical illustrations together with the critical comment was at first considered and then discarded. It would offer no solution whatsoever for the majority of our readers, since your average music lover, unfortunately, is not sufficiently literate in musical symbols, while the trained musician can easily gain access to the full scores if his curiosity is sufficiently whetted.

To overcome this obstacle, the author has prepared an appendix in which are listed phonograph recordings of the major works (or portions of works) discussed in the book. It is hoped that the music lover, after reading this book, will make an effort to hear through the gramophone the music that has been discussed here. There are libraries in major cities which have facilities for hearing records free of charge; in New York City, for example, the branch at Fifty-eighth Street near Lexington Avenue has a remarkably comprehensive collection of records available to everyone. Or, if the reader is himself a collector of records, it is hoped that he will enrich his own library by purchasing at least a

[6]

few of those items that are listed in the appendix, so that he can refer to them again and again while reading this book. Records can vitalize this book for the reader, and make the subject of old music alive and absorbing.

Many composers discussed in this book are not merely of historic importance. Though they have been brushed aside by the world of music and forgotten by it, composers like Kuhnau, Dittersdorf, John Field, Johann Stamitz and Buxtehude belong in our concert halls. It was, therefore, one of the goals of the author in preparing this book—together with giving the layman an acquaintance with some of the less well-known forces in musical history—to help direct some light to a few forgotten masters. To become acquainted with their best works, as this writer has done, is to come into contact with music of transcendent quality, music that has feeling, intensity, depth and beauty.

No doubt these forgotten composers will eventually come into their own, just as other forgotten composers of the past have been restored in recent decades through the heroic missionary work of Arnold Dolmetsch, Henri Casadesus and Wanda Landowska. But the reader of this book can help advance the date of their recognition by a decade, or by several decades, if —on his own—he will explore some of this neglected music through phonograph records. He will discover music which, at its best, reaches toward the highest plane of artistic expression, which becomes (as one writer so felicitously remarked about all great music) "a matrix of the absolute."

A page from a recent edition of Caccini's *Euridice*

(Notice the increased decorations of the melodic line)

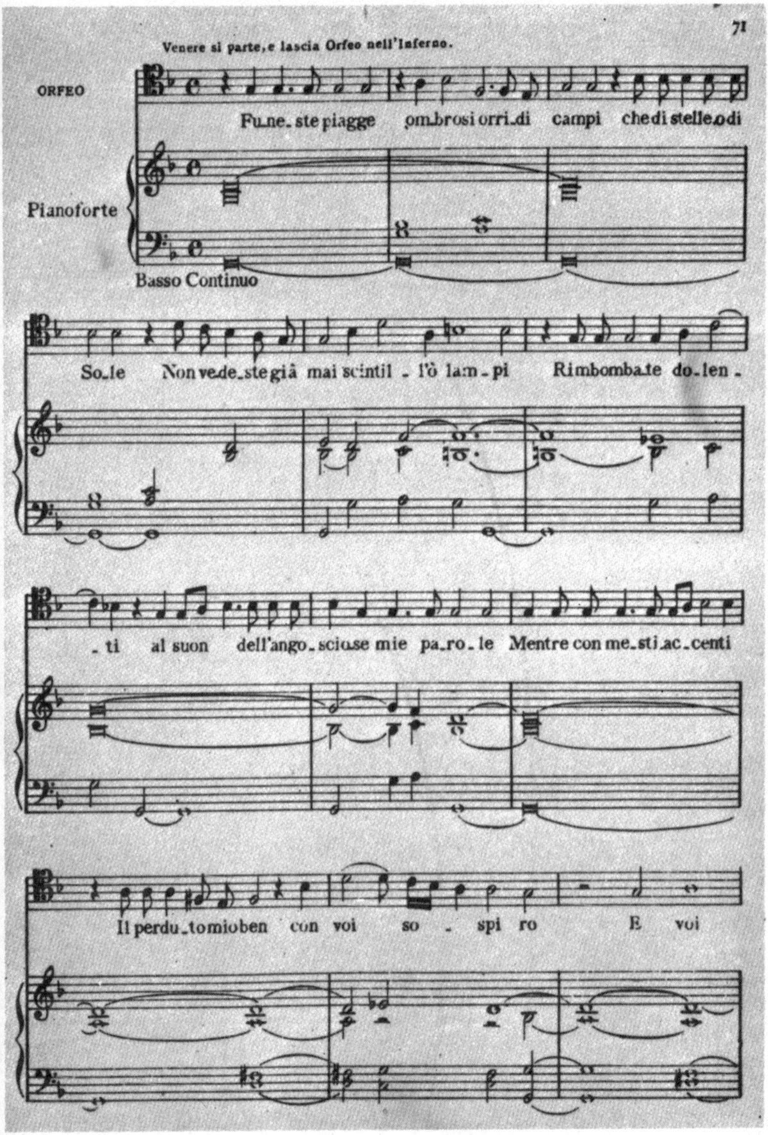

A page from a recent edition of Peri's *Euridice*

L'ORFEO

FAVOLA IN MVSICA

DA CLAVDIO MONTEVERDI

RAPPRESENTATA IN MANTOVA

l'Anno 1607. & nouamente data in luce.

AL SERENISSIMO SIGNOR

D. FRANCESCO GONZAGA

Prencipe di Mantoua , & di Monferato , &c.

In Venetia Appreſſo Ricciardo Amadino.

M D C I X.

The title page from the first edition (1609) of
Monteverdi's *Orfeo*

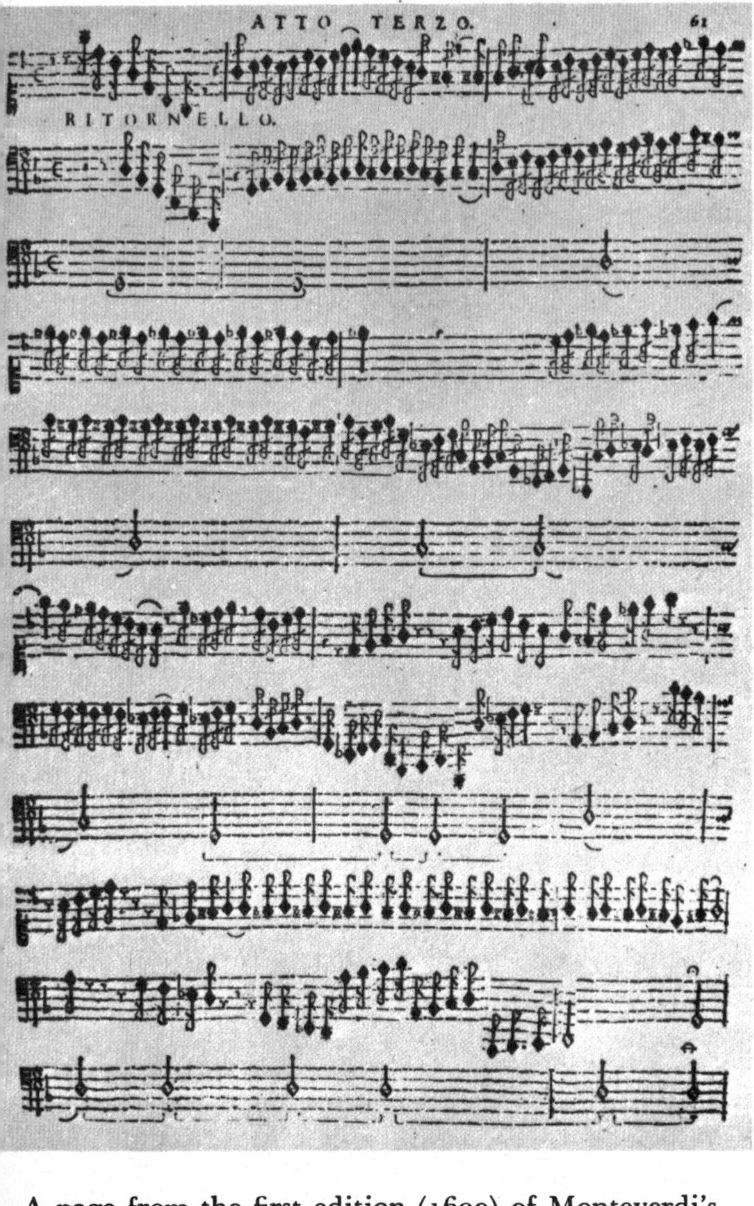

A page from the first edition (1609) of Monteverdi's *Orfeo*

Jean Philippe Rameau

Christoph Willibald Gluck

Heinrich Schütz

Alessandro Scarlatti

Pietro Trapassi Metastasio

Giacomo Durazzo

I

THE EARLY OPERA AND ORATORIO

TOWARD the close of the sixteenth century in
Florence, Italy, a group of dilettanti met regularly at the home of Giovanni Bardi, nobleman, patron and art lover, to discuss questions pertaining to
art. In their discussions they were, of course, influenced
by the Renaissance which had already contributed its
greatest riches to Florence and which had already
passed its zenith. The great Florentine spirits of the
Renaissance—Donatello, Michelangelo, Leonardo da
Vinci, Benvenuto Cellini—were dead. Dead, and yet
how alive!—for Florence was still fresh with their
memories. In a niche of the Cathedral façade stood
Donatello's *St. John the Evangelist;* near the entrance
of the City Hall loomed the figure of Michelangelo's
David. These, and innumerable other creations of Florentine genius, were everywhere—keeping alive the last
burning fires of the Renaissance.

The spirit of the Renaissance, which a half century
earlier had made the city throb with artistic and intel-

lectual life, had not yet entirely subsided. And it was acutely felt by this group of Florentine dilettanti who —in or about 1580—gathered to talk about music and the theatre.

This group of dilettanti is referred to by musical history as the "camerata." Its intellectual leaders were Giovanni Bardi and the nobleman Jacopo Corsi, another patron of art; both of them occasionally dabbled in the writing of poetry and music. The others included Vincenzo Galilei (father of the world-famous scientist), an amateur composer and a talented performer on the lute and viol; Giulio Caccini, Jacopo Peri and Emilio del Cavalieri, all three of them reputable composers; Ottavio Rinuccini, a poet; and several others distinguished in the artistic life of the city.

Inspired by the Renaissance, the "camerata" turned to the culture and particularly to the art and literature of the ancient Greeks in their many discussions. The group had seen (so they argued among themselves) the revival of Greek learning and of Greek plastic art. Why, they demanded, should not an effort be made to restore, as well, the dignity and majesty of the classic Greek drama?

To restore this dignity, the "camerata" hit upon the ingenious idea of using a collaboration of music and drama. ("In the opinion of many," said Peri, "the Greeks *sang* the whole of their tragedies on the stage.") But the members of the "camerata" realized that the music then in the vogue was altogether inadequate for their purpose. The music of the time was vocal rather than instrumental, and in the vocal music, polyphony (or the simultaneous use of several independent voices of equal importance) was the favored style. It was the late sixteenth century, and opera, orchestral music, chamber music, even important works for solo instruments other than the organ, had not yet been born. Music's most prominent place was in the church, where elaborate vocal settings were parts of the service. There was secular vocal music as well—mostly madrigals (also polyphonic in style) in which composers translated idyllic poetic subjects into music light in character and treatment. The instruments of the time included the lute, the virginal or clavier (forerunners of the piano), the organ, and such stringed instruments as the old viols. But all these instruments, except for the organ, were used primarily to accompany the voice; composers had not yet learned (except in rare and unimportant intervals) that significant solo music could be written for them. And when composers wrote for the organ, or when they wrote instrumental music for combinations of viols, the music they produced was invariably polyphonic—as if they were writing for groupings of human voices and not for instruments.

In directing a critical eye on the music of its own day, the "camerata" argued that such music was poorly suited for the goal they had in mind: the restoration of the Greek tragedy through the union of music and drama. Polyphony, said the members of the "camerata," was too cumbersome, too confusing; above all else, it failed to articulate clearly the text—and without clear articulation how could a successful union of words and music be achieved?

> The one thing everyone agreed upon [wrote the seventeenth century Florentine, Giovanni Battista Doni] was that since the music of the day was quite inadequate to the expression of the words, and in its development repugnant to the thought, means must be found in the attempt to bring music closer to that of the classical times, and to bring out the chief melody prominently so that the poetry should be clearly understandable.

What they needed was a new music that was a radical departure from anything that had yet been known.

What type of music they were seeking was not quite clear to them until they came upon a Greek treatise on music written by Aristoxenus. Aristoxenus believed that speech should be used as a model for song. A music that aped the inflection of human speech could make the verse intelligible—the solution was as efficacious as it was simple. Besides, such music was single-voiced, and could become the expression of an *individual* (which would be needed in the theatre); and the multiple-voiced polyphony could only suggest the masses.

> Place no value upon music which makes it impossible to understand the words [wrote the composer Giulio Caccini, one of the leading spirits of the "camerata"]. Such music only destroys the unity and meter and sometimes lengthens them in order to suit the counterpoint. This is a real mangling of the poetry. On the other hand . . . hold to the principle so greatly extolled by Plato and the other philosophers: "Let music be first of all language and rhythm, and secondly, tone; but not vice-versa."

To the composer Peri, specifically to the detailed introduction with which he prefaced his opera *Eu-*

ridice, we owe our knowledge of the birth of the new revolutionary musical style. The phrasing of his text is sometimes awkward, and the style cumbersome; but the introduction is an illuminating document.

It pleased Signor Corsi and Rinuccini (in the year 1594) to have me set to music the play of *Dafne* . . . treating it in a new manner. I was to show by a simple experiment of what the song of our age is capable. I decided that I must accordingly seek in my music to imitate one who speaks. . . . For it seemed to me that ancient Greeks and Romans . . . must have made use of a sort of music which, while surpassing the sounds of ordinary speech, fell far short of the melody of singing, and assumed the shape of something intermediate between the two. . . .

Therefore, abandoning every style of vocal writing hitherto known, I gave myself up wholly to contriving the sort of imitation demanded by this poem. And, considering that the sort of vocal delivery applied by the ancients to singing . . . could be somewhat accelerated, so as to hold a mean course between the slow and deliberate pace of singing and the nimble, rapid pace of speaking (thus making it serve my purpose); considering this, I also recognized that, in our speech, some sounds are intoned in such a way that harmony can be based upon them. I also recognized that we pass through other sounds in speech which are not so intoned until we return to the one which is capable of forming a new consonance. And, having regard for the accents and modes of expression we use (in grief, rejoicing, and so on), I made the bass move at a rate appropriate to them, now faster, now slower, according to the emotions that were expressed. And I sustained the bass through both dissonances and consonances, until the speaker's voice, after passing through various degrees of pitch, comes to those sounds which, being intoned in ordinary speech, facilitate the formation of a new consonance.

Thus the recitative, the spine of the early opera, came into being, evolved through the discussions of a group of intellectual figures in Florence. The recitative, as the "camerata" conceived it, was music that (as Peri wrote) imitated "one who speaks"; it was declamation accompanied by lutes or harpsichord or organ. Theory soon made way for practice. As early as 1590, Emilio del Cavalieri wrote musical scenes or pastorals called *Il Satiro* and *La disperazione di Fileno,* believed to be the first time that the new style had been employed—and ten years before Cavalieri himself was to charter a new course for the recitative with the oratorio. Galilei created monodic settings of the *Lamentations of Jeremiah* and translated the Ugolino scene from Dante's *Divine Comedy* into recitative.

But the recitative, or *stilo rappresentativo,* was not the final goal of the "camerata." They sought to restore the Greek classic drama, not to evolve a new style of musical composition. Guided by their ideals, the members of Bardi's intellectual circle brought the recitative into the theatre.

The first of them to set a dramatic work entirely to recitatives was Jacopo Peri, in a work which he composed in 1594 and which he aptly designated as a *dramma per musica,* a work entitled *Dafne.* Peri, in composing *Dafne,* had hoped to revive the classic Greek drama. What he actually succeeded in doing was to evolve an altogether new art form. That art form was later to be known as the "opera."

The predecessors of *Dafne*—spoken of by the musical historian as "the first opera"—were the early dramatic forms, both secular and religious, such as the Italian intermezzo, the allegorical festival plays, the masques, the old masquerades, open-air church fêtes. These, and other early dramatic forms, called upon music, from time to time, to supplement the dramatic action on the stage and to give it greater emphasis. But *Dafne* was the first dramatic work which was set *throughout* to music; and because of this its composer has earned the distinction of being the first opera composer in musical history.

Jacopo Peri—his friends playfully nicknamed him *Il Zazzerino* because of his long hair—was born in Florence on August 20, 1561 of noble lineage. Under the competent instruction of Cristofano Malvezzi, a canon and Kapellmeister well respected in Florence, he received a comprehensive musical education. In 1601, Peri was called to the court of Ferrara, an indication that his reputation had penetrated beyond his native city. And no wonder! *Dafne,* which Peri had composed in 1594, had become so popular after its first private performance that repeated presentations were given during the carnivals of 1597, 1598, and 1599.

[*19*]

The new theatrical form pleased its audiences, for it had both novelty and dramatic interest; and its originator became greatly honored.

The score of *Dafne* has been lost. Yet from what we know of Peri's later opera, *Euridice* (which has survived), we can recreate for ourselves the epoch-making evening when the first performance of the first opera took place.

The scene is a salon in Jacopo Corsi's palace in Florence. The small auditorium is crowded with the leading intellectual figures of Florence as well as with several members of nobility. The members of the "camerata" are there, impatient to see a practical realization of their theories. The composer, Peri, is backstage, putting on his costume—for he is performing one of the principal roles, that of Apollo.

The salon darkens; the curtains part. A simple play unfolds, told with the literalness of a nursery book. Dafne, the beloved of Apollo, is pursued by the god. To protect Dafne, her mother changes her into a laurel tree which henceforth becomes sacred to Apollo. This is the whole story. The various characters appear on the stage and recite their poetic lines with exaggerated inflections, and they are accompanied by a small orchestra that includes a harpsichord, lyres, lutes. There is a chorus and a ballet, but these are not integral parts of the play but are used with sparing economy by the composer to inject an occasional touch of variety.

The select audience at Jacopo Corsi's palace is delighted by a new aesthetic experience, and it expresses its enthusiasm without restraint. Encouraged by the reception given his first major work, and warmed by the sincere enthusiasm of his friends of the "camerata," Peri decided to compose a second dramatic work in music, *Euridice*—for the festivities held in Florence attending the marriage of Henry IV of France to Maria de' Medici on February 9, 1600.

For the first time, a theme so well loved by opera composers is treated in dramatic-musical form: the well-known story of Orpheus and Eurydice. But like Gluck, many years later, Peri was to permit tampering with the classic tale, to allow for a happy ending. The marriage festivities of Henry IV were not to be marred by a tragic story which permanently kept Orpheus and Eurydice apart!

With this second work, Peri became one of the best known of Florentine composers. His soaring reputation brought him the most important post of his career, court musician in Ferrara.

Of Peri's later career, only one significant fact need

[*21*]

be noted. In 1608, he collaborated with Monteverdi (still another indication of his reputation with his contemporaries) in the writing of *Arianna,* a *dramma per musica,* for which Peri wrote the recitatives and Monteverdi the arias. Other musical works which Peri wrote later in life added little to his importance. He died in Florence on August 12, 1633.

The second dramatic-musical setting of the story of Orpheus and Eurydice (on the very text of Rinuccini used by Peri) was the work of another member of the "camerata," Giulio Caccini. Caccini's *Euridice* was first published in 1600, and parts of it were interpolated into Peri's work during the latter's first performance.

If the friends of the "camerata" nicknamed Peri the "long-haired one," they might very aptly have spoken of Caccini as the "immodest one." Few composers have had so glowing an appreciation of their own talent as Caccini, and few have had his lack of reticence in singing hymns of self-adulation.

> Neither in ancient nor in modern times [Caccini has said with too eloquent directness], so far as I know, has music of such transcendent beauty ever existed as that which I hear resounding in my soul.

Caccini was born in Rome in or about 1550. He received his early training in singing from Scipione della Palla, for from boyhood he had a beautiful voice. Caccini came to Florence in 1564 to become court-singer and lutist to the Grand Duke of Tuscany. Some years later, he associated himself with the "camerata" and was given by his friends a new artistic direction. After composing *Euridice*, on the model set by Peri, Caccini published in 1602 a still more significant work. It was the monumental work, *Nuove musiche*, a set of monodies, which was epoch-making in causing a definite break with the old school of polyphony by establishing and crystallizing the new style of writing melodies. Caccini's influence was far-reaching.

> It must be confessed [wrote Doni] that we owe to him, in a great measure, the new and graceful manner of singing which at that time spread over Italy.

Thereafter, Caccini devoted himself to the theatre, and composed several works—such as the *Combattimento d'Apolline col serpente,* and (in collaboration with Peri) *Il ratto di Cefale*—which further established the musical drama as an art form. Giulio Caccini died in Florence on December 10, 1618.

Caccini, like Peri, wrote with an almost stark simplicity. The characters appear on the stage and (as in the Peri operas) indulge in declamation of speeches accompanied by the strumming of instruments. Of melodies, singable, tuneful melodies, there is not the slightest trace.

What can the present-day critic say of either Peri or Caccini beyond pointing to their historic importance? The music of transcendent beauty which Caccini found in his soul is, unfortunately, not in the pages of his score. Fingering page after page of recitatives, one succeeding the other in dull sequence and only occasionally, and all too infrequently, interrupted by a brief piece for chorus or ballet, brings small aesthetic compensation to a twentieth century music lover. Jules Combarieu speaks of the "monotony," the "gaps," and the "false vocal ornaments" of Caccini's *Euridice;* the criticism might even more justifiably be made of Peri, who had an even duller melodic line than Caccini. The truth is that to the twentieth century musician the two operas about Orpheus and Eurydice have painful restrictions. They are dull, without feeling or life. The composers had not yet learned to use the resources of either voice or accompaniment. There is no attempt at theatrical effect, and most certainly little of emotional appeal.

And yet both Peri and Caccini were pioneers—bold and adventurous—of whom the history of music may well be proud. They sensed what the role of the musical drama should be, for they frequently insisted that the music they wrote should interpret the text. Sometimes there is an attempt at tone painting, in their fumbling attempt to find the proper lyric line or the proper interval with which to depict a certain line of verse.

Caccini, more than Peri, gave the voice a certain measure of freedom it had never before known. His writing is ornate (for being a singer and a singing master he was proud of the flexibility of the human voice). But Caccini realized a homophonic style, supporting his florid voice part with a simple chordal accompaniment; and for this alone history must be grateful to him.

We might well repeat what one French critic [1] wrote of Caccini:

Let us permit the *Nuove musiche* and *Euridice* to rest quietly in their eternal sleep, and

[1] Robert Marchal, in *La Revue musicale,* February, 1925.

let us not do Caccini the evil service of awakening them. But let us remember that their author was a workman of first importance, and that he pointed out a direction to those who followed him . . . which worthier and stronger souls than he were to enrich and ennoble.

The *dramma per musica* did not wait long for the first of these "worthier and stronger souls." He was Claudio Monteverdi, one of the unquestioned masters of music, and one of its significant pioneers. Monteverdi's genius converted an amorphous form into a vibrant work of art. It was Monteverdi who first suggested, and to a certain extent realized, the full artistic possibilities of the new art-form, giving it direction and significance. For an achievement of such scope a composer requires, together with creative imagination, a vision, the boldness of an adventurer, the self-assurance of a master. And these qualities belonged to Monteverdi.

Unlike so many other musicians of the seventeenth century, he could not shake works out of his sleeve. Others might manufacture one work after another to a convenient and adaptable matrix. He was, above everything else, the craftsman who was artist, and the artist-craftsman. He fashioned each and every work meticulously to its own measurements and design. He wrote copiously; but whatever he wrote came from him after long and fastidious preparation.

Temperamentally, he was unsuited for the age of patronage which demanded from its hirelings musical works on order, often tailor-made to specifications. He was frequently in despair—sometimes even made violently ill—by the insistent commissions of his patrons who preferred facility and superficiality to painstaking and meticulous composition. "I do most heartily pray your Most Serene Highness, for the love of God, no longer to put so much work on me and to give me more time for my great desire to serve you," he was once forced to write to his employer. "Otherwise the excess of my fatigue will not fail to shorten my life."

His only existing portrait shows a somber face. The lips are pressed hard together. The eyes are grave and severe. His letters further suggest these motives of somberness and gravity. For, truth to tell, he was a man who had suffered greatly throughout his life. Yet suffering—which often came in the form of intense physical pain—could not weaken his formidable powers of creation. He was a composer, first and foremost (though he did love art and literature passionately, and sometimes even dabbled in alchemy). Composing was as essential to him as breathing and eating. We know that he was always working at his music, with an enormous capacity for concentration and devotion to his task. But he worked hard because work meant creation, and in creating he was as oblivious to time and fatigue as he was to his personal sufferings.

He was the modernist of his time. His unresolved discords created as much dismay and confusion among sixteenth century pundits as Schönberg's atonality has done in our own time. Did not Artusi, a gifted musician in his own rights, sneer at his music as appealing more to the senses than to reason? Monteverdi refused to be a slave to convention or to tradition. As he so boldly and unequivocally wrote in the preface of his fifth book of madrigals, there existed for him a system of harmony other than that formulated by Zarlino, a system based on enriched resources and new effects.

His restless intellect always groped for a new manner of expressing itself, just as it was always searching for stimulation in classic literature (Plato particularly) and in the great works of art. One of his works, the *Canzonette a tre voci*, published in 1584, already boldly used dissonances, particularly the dominant seventh and ninth chords. His friends and relatives first diagnosed this as the impetuousness of his youth, and felt that he would soon outgrow these artistic wild oats. But they reckoned without Monteverdi's inexhaustible passion for discovering new ideas and new idioms. Even in his last work, *L'Incoronazione di Poppea*—the first historic play in music—he was still experimenting with new devices, and groping for new methods of approaching musical realism.

He was always sensitively alive to the new forms and styles which were arising in different parts of Europe; and he was always ready to adopt them when he felt that they could serve his artistic ends. Though he retained his own identity as a composer throughout his life—and that identity revealed itself in the deep feeling and in the powerful dramatic impact of all his music—he was always sufficiently progressive in assimilating new methods. In 1599, when he traveled to Flanders in the company of his employer, the Duke of Mantua, he came into contact with the French school of composers. He studied their style and technique and soon adapted their more rhythmic manner of vocal writing to his own madrigals, motets and songs—the first Italian to do so. Once again, in 1600, when Peri's *Euridice* came to his attention he was sufficiently perceptive to realize that a new age had arisen for music, and sufficiently adventurous to discard his past and to become a part of that new age. In comparison with this new form, he saw, the madrigal which he had employed until now with such supreme technical skill and independence appeared painfully restricted. With the freedom of a truly liberated spirit, he was prepared to enter upon a new phase of his creative life.

Claudio Monteverdi was born in Cremona on May 15, 1567. His father, a physician, had strong sympathy for the arts which he transferred to his sons. From Marcantonio Ingegneri—the eminent theorist, composer and organist of Cremona—Monteverdi received a comprehensive musical education. In 1583, he proved the thoroughness of his training with his first publication, spiritual madrigals for four voices.

In 1589, Monteverdi became violist in the court orchestra of Duke Vincenzo in Mantua, at a monthly income of twelve and a half crowns—a respectable salary, though it was hardly sufficient to provide for Monteverdi that style of life which the Duke demanded of all his employees. But there were other compensations. The Duke had fashioned himself after the patrons of the Renaissance. He loved and encouraged music, the theatre, the ballet, balls, art. Perhaps through his influence, Mantua was one of the cultural centers of Italy at that time. In such a setting, there was no little intellectual stimulation for a young and sensitive musician.

In 1601, Monteverdi was elevated to the post of master of the chapel by Duke Vincenzo. His salary was less adequate than before; and—worse luck still!—it was not always collectible without a squabble. It has been recorded that on one occasion Monteverdi was compelled to enter into hot dispute with the treasurer for the salary that was due him. And a poor salary was coupled with exacting work. For a composer like Monteverdi who could work only slowly and fastidiously, the demands made on him by his employer frequently brought on illness, unhappiness and morbidity. Yet he was a composer who could not permit personal affliction to stand in the way of his artistic creation. In spite of the unhappy circumstances of his life, inspiration was not to be thwarted. He was to pass from one wonderful period of his career, that of his madrigals, to another still more wonderful, that of the *dramma per musica*. In 1605, he published his fifth book of madrigals, in which he brought the madrigal form to its highest Italian development. Thereafter, he was to travel in the unexplored territory of the music-play—

where he was to clear so much ground and which he was to make so much more habitable for the composers who followed him.

He had first heard of the Florentine "camerata" and their evolution of a new dramatic form when he returned from his travels in Flanders in 1599. It is generally believed that, one year later, he attended a performance of Peri's *Euridice;* at any rate, he most certainly acquainted himself with the new work. Peri's drama moved him profoundly, for he recognized at once what limitless possibilities the new form might offer a composer with a strong dramatic vein for writing. That it was a few years before such a work was finally created was only due to the fact that Monteverdi was always the slow and fastidious worker.

The *dramma per musica,* as Monteverdi received it from Peri and Caccini, lacked cohesion. The recitative was used to carry the narrative, and an occasional show-piece for the voice or a decorative dance interrupted the story to provide some variety for eye and ear. But there was no attempt to integrate music and drama into a unified texture. Nor was there a definite artistic purpose, a definite understanding of what the new form was competent to achieve. In the *Euridice* of each

[*32*]

composer, drama took precedence over music. There was also misplaced overemphasis on scenic painter and dancer, rather than on singer and orchestra. And these abuses were combined with poverty of musical resources.

Yet with little example to guide him, Monteverdi created an *Orfeo.* . . .

Orfeo—the libretto was prepared by Alessandro Striggio—was first presented before a small circle at a meeting of the Accademia degli Invaghiti. This took place at the royal palace of Mantua on February 24, 1607.

Orfeo was a pronounced success (as the poet, Ferrari, hastened to inform the Duke by letter), for no great perception was required on the part of that small audience to recognize the many new sluices opened by Monteverdi for the new theatrical form. In comparison with a work so rich in invention, and so fully realized, as *Orfeo* was, the works of Peri and Caccini appeared archaic. Monteverdi's recitative was the recitative of Peri and Caccini—but, the difference! The humdrum and stilted monodic line had suddenly acquired flexibility, texture, artistic meaning. There were subtle modulations and genuine dramatic impact. A greater independence of movement conveyed deep feeling of emotion. There was, however, much more than recitative in this Monteverdi opera. For the first time an aria was being evolved. At his best, Monteverdi achieved a lyric line that set a standard for melodic writing: the eloquent *Ecco pur ch'à voi ritorno* which opens the second act must have touched more than one heart at that first performance. Yet there were not only arias in *Orfeo* but even duets and trios.

In place of a primitive orchestra, consisting of a group of lutes supplemented by a keyboard instrument, used by Peri and Caccini, there was for Monteverdi's opera an orchestra of more than thirty musicians, including violins, viole da braccia, viole da gamba and bass viols, harpsichord, organ, harp, flute, cornets, sackbuts (trombones), chittaroni (large lutes), and so on. This accompanying orchestra became with Monteverdi an essential part of the drama; not just a mere strumming obbligato. New devices were invented for it by Monteverdi, such as the pizzicato and the tremolo to suggest dramatic excitement.

The orchestra was used by Monteverdi not only to intensify the drama on the stage, but—as in his introduction and the *ritornelli*—also to set a mood for the action that was to follow. In such orchestral passages, Monteverdi wrote with the same sound instincts, infallible taste and resourcefulness that he brought to the voice. Just as he evolved for the singers a vocal style of which Peri and Caccini may have dreamt but never realized, so for the orchestra he was one of the first composers to realize successfully a truly instrumental style; or, as one critic remarked,[1] he wrote for the orchestra

> music which is possible only on string instruments—music in which the interest is that of harmony, texture, and tone color, and is completely independent of imitative movement of parts.

And while writing for his orchestra, Monteverdi enriched the equipment of harmony with such fertility that some have since called him the father of modern harmony. No longer does an elementary chordal accompaniment support the voice. In *Orfeo* there is a rich orchestration of sound, with deep inner voices, bringing additional personality to the music; and dissonance is used (just as it was used earlier in his madrigals) to inject color.

But most important of all, in *Orfeo* music and text are of almost equal importance, each sharing the bur-

[1] Adam Carse, in *The Sackbut,* 1921.

den of projecting the drama, each contributing to the other new qualities of expression. Thus, *Orfeo* was the first drama in music to realize the artistic possibilities of the new form conceived by Peri, and to give that form significance. As Henri Prunières wrote in his biography of the composer,

> he turned the aristocratic spectacle of Florence into modern musical drama, overflowing with life and bearing in its mighty waves of sound the passions which make up the human soul.

On May 28, 1608, one year after the presentation of *Orfeo,* a second Monteverdi drama in music, *Arianna,* was produced at the theatre in the Castle of Mantua before an audience of several thousand, and with a cast including leading singers from Mantua and Florence. Of *Arianna* only one excerpt has survived, but, fortunately, so extraordinary is the power of its emotion that, once again, the work of Peri and Caccini is ridiculously dwarfed. This is the famous *Lament of Arianna,* one of the most moving pieces of music composed before the time of Bach. It is known that before he composed his *Lament,* Monteverdi lost his wife; possibly, he expressed his own grief in this throbbing, eloquent excerpt. We are told by one of Monteverdi's contemporaries that when this piece was first heard, it "visibly moved the entire theatre to tears." That capacity to move the heart has not been lost from Monteverdi's *"Lament."* It remains an unforgettable example of early lyric writing—fresh, simple, eloquent.

In 1612, Monteverdi left Mantua for Venice, and in 1613 he became the master of the chapel at St. Mark's at the unusual salary of five hundred ducats a year. He was now the most famous musician in Europe, and was accorded in Venice that homage which was due him. In 1633, Monteverdi embraced priesthood—probably in gratitude for having escaped untouched by the Venetian plague of 1630. Until the end of his life he remained in Venice leading a simple, monastic existence in what approximated a monk's cell. He consecrated his life more than ever to his many musical duties. He trained the choir, played the organ, taught his pupils, and composed music.

In the closing years of his life, he had grown riper as a composer. For Venice he composed many remarkable dramatic works. (At least eight of his later compositions for the theatre have disappeared.) His style lost none of its dignity but, on the other hand, grew richer and more mellow; and his necessity to seek out the new remained as great. The justly famous *L'Incoronazione di Poppea,* first performed in Venice one year before his death, is an eloquent testimony to his ever-increasing powers as a composer. In this, his last work, there are passages which may well be said to rank with the greatest of his music—the exquisite lullaby sung by Poppea's attendant maid, *Oblivion soave,* or the famous Octavia scene with its sharp dramatic writing.[1] Thus, like Michelangelo, to whom he has often been compared, Monteverdi grew artistically deeper with old age, and died when he was virtually at the height of his powers.

The *dramma per musica* quickly rose in popularity. The people found it to be a novel and exciting form of entertainment, and took to it. The first performances of these early dramas in music were given by itinerant companies of singers and musicians who came into town by cart and performed several times a day in the public square. Crowds would eagerly await the arrival of the company, then would express their enthusiasm with hoarse shouts of acclaim, demanding repetitions

---

[1] *L'Incoronazione di Poppea* is not altogether unknown to American music audiences. During 1932–1933 it was revived by the students of the Juilliard School, in New York, in an edited version by Vincent D'Indy. It was also featured, in a new edition by Ernest Krenek, by the Salzburg Opera Guild in its tour of this country.

of those scenes that particularly struck their fancy. For the masses this new dramatic-musical form had such an appeal that, as Pietro della Valle recorded, many of them even

> continued following our cart to ten or twelve different places where it stopped, and never quitted us as long as we remained in the street, which was from four o'clock in the evening until after midnight.

From performances in the public square to those in a theatre founded expressly for these dramas in music was but a short step. It was not long before the first such theatre came into existence. The San Cassiano Theatre—which opened in the year 1637 in Venice with (appropriately enough!) a new work by Monteverdi, *Adone*—was the first opera house. The boxes were rented annually by the high-born of Venetian society, as well as by foreign princes; for the universality of the new theatrical form embraced high and low alike. The general public could gain admission into the spacious parterre by paying approximately twenty cents a head.

The new theatre was a tremendous success. German princes retained theatre boxes for themselves from year to year so that they might visit the theatre regularly and keep in touch with all the new dramatic-musical forms. Between 1641 and 1649, no less than thirty different works in music, some of which were Monteverdi's, were played.

The term "opera" has not been used for the works of Peri, Caccini or Monteverdi for, truth to tell, it was first with Cavalli, Monteverdi's pupil, that the name made an appearance. Cavalli's first dramatic work in music, *Le nozze di Teti*—composed in 1639—was called by him an *opera-scenica*. The art-form conceived by the Florentine "camerata" was now—though somewhat belatedly—to receive its baptismal name.

Cavalli (his original name was Pietro Francesco Caletti-Bruni) was born in Crema on February 14, 1602. When the Podestà of Crema, Fredrico Cavalli, offered to sponsor and finance the musical career of young Caletti-Bruni, the boy's name was officially changed to that of his patron.

Cavalli's father was the choirmaster of the town of Crema. From him the boy first received lessons in music. After he had been adopted by the Podestà, the boy was sent to Venice to become a singer in the choir of St. Mark's, at the same time becoming a pupil of Monteverdi. In 1617, Cavalli was registered as a tenor in St. Mark's. In 1640, he was its organist, and in 1668 he became the master of the chapel.

During this long period of activity in Venice, Cavalli took several trips to Paris. In 1660, he was invited there to help in the production of his opera *Xerse* which formed a part of the marriage festivities of Louis XIV. He was back in Paris two years later, this time to assist in the presentation of his opera, *Ercole amante,* which celebrated the Peace of the Pyrenees. Thus Cavalli was instrumental in bringing the Italian opera to France and the channel through which the Italian influence was passed on to the first French composers of opera.

Francesco Cavalli died in Venice on January 14, 1676. He had been one of the most celebrated composers of his time; the pupil had become the successor of his teacher not only as the master of the chapel in St. Mark's but also as one of the leading creators of Italian opera.

More clearly even than Monteverdi, Cavalli made a distinction between recitative and aria, giving to each more of the character it was to adopt with the later Italians: the recitative became an expressive medium for dramatic pronouncements—sharp, concise; and the aria received from him an enrichment of treatment and greater decorative elegance than it had previously known.[1] Cavalli also went a step further than Monteverdi in using his orchestra for tone-color and dramatic effects.

He was Monteverdi's successor, but his stature was smaller than that of his teacher. For all his inventive facility, he had none of Monteverdi's adventurousness, none of Monteverdi's compulsion to seek out new ways of expressing himself. No doubt there is great justification in Romain Rolland's statement that Cavalli's genius dominated "the whole of Italian opera in the seventeenth century"; for Cavalli was studied and aped by an entire generation of opera composers who modeled their music after his. Yet—though we recognize Cavalli's significance—we must also confess that in certain important respects Cavalli departed from the path of his master, and not to the advantage of the opera form. At his best, Monteverdi groped for something more ambitious than a musical entertainment to please the senses. He dreamed of that powerful dramatic-musical form which was ultimately to be realized with Gluck. But Cavalli, a victim of his own remarkable capacity

[1] *Grove's Dictionary of Music and Musicians,* vol. 1, gives an excellent example of Cavalli's melodic gifts, with an excerpt from *Il Giasone.*

[*42*]

for lyric writing, made the opera a showcase in which to display his jewel-like melodies. More and more he directed opera towards those formal and stilted patterns which were to be smugly accepted by so many later Italians.

Those more formal patterns were next developed in Naples by one of the most richly endowed composers in the early history of music. Alessandro Scarlatti wrote in almost every form of music, and every form was filled with the abundance of his ideas. To opera, chamber music, and oratorio alike he brought his inexhaustible melodic invention and his capacity to create beauty. He did not bring structural development to the forms he employed; no new vistas were opened by him. The technique and forms of his predecessors satisfied him, for they proved efficacious in lighting a spark to the fuse of his inexhaustible imagination.

He was the founder of the Neapolitan school of opera which succeeded the Venetian school of Monteverdi and Cavalli. He was born in Palermo in 1659, and his study of music took place in Rome—possibly under Carissimi, the father of the oratorio, though Romain Rolland has gone to some pains to refute this. In Rome, Scarlatti's first opera was performed (the year was 1679) and it aroused the admiration of Christina, the ex-Queen of Sweden, who endowed him for a short period.

In 1682, Scarlatti decided to join several members of his family who had previously settled in Naples. There he remained for the next twenty years. In 1684, he succeeded Andrea Ziani as Kapellmeister and presented his first two operas to Neapolitan audiences. For the next few years, he composed copiously for the stage. These works were performed regularly both at the royal palace and at the San Bartolomeo Theatre, and exerted a powerful influence on those who heard them. Composers in Naples began to imitate them; they were encouraged by the examples set by Scarlatti to compose abundantly in a similar vein. Thus it was not long before Naples became a center of operatic activity just as Venice had been some years earlier.

Just as Scarlatti's operas became the models for other composers in Naples, so the Neapolitan opera became the model for other Italian composers everywhere—and not only during the seventeenth century but in the eighteenth as well. As Charles Burney commented:

> I find part of his [Scarlatti's] property among the stolen goods of all the best composers of the

first forty or fifty years of the eighteenth century.

Political disturbances in Naples brought Scarlatti to the northern part of Italy in 1702. He came with the hope of gaining the patronage of Ferdinand III, the son of the Grand Duke of Tuscany, and a famous Florentine music lover, but, unfortunately, Scarlatti's musical style did not appeal. From Florence, Scarlatti went on to Rome. There he met Cardinal Ottoboni (the famous patron of Corelli) through whose influence Scarlatti was appointed assistant musical director of Santa Maria Maggiore. In Rome, Scarlatti continued the writing of operas: by 1705, he had completed his eighty-eighth dramatic work!

In or about 1713, encouraged by an offer of the office of Kapellmeister, Scarlatti returned to Naples. He now remained there until the end of his life, working hard during these years, and producing abundantly.

In the course of last week [commented the *Gazzetta di Napoli* of October 30, 1725], there died the celebrated Cavaliere Alessandro Scarlatti, to whom music owes much for the numerous works with which he enriched it.

[45]

"To whom music owes much" . . . In Scarlatti's works, the opera form assumes more closely the recognizable features of the later Italian opera. The librettos become filled, more and more, with unreal situations, sawdust characters, and pompous showmanship. The aria, of which Scarlatti was one of the greatest early masters, became even more ornamental than it had been with Cavalli.

And yet (as his own contemporaries were not slow to realize) he was a force of great importance; and his contributions were many. He developed the "Italian overture" (or sinfonia), in which two fast sections are separated by a slow one—which might well be considered a forerunner of the symphony. He is also responsible for the *da capo* aria (which, in his hands, became an instrument capable of great elegance), and the orchestrally accompanied recitative. He made adroit use of ensemble singing. These are significant details. But, more important still, Scarlatti

gathered up all that was best of the tangled materials produced by that age of transition and experiment, the seventeenth century, to form out of them a musical language, vigorous and

[*46*]

flexible as Italian itself, which has been the foundation of all music of the classical period.[1]

In short, Scarlatti crystallized the operatic formula which future composers were to adopt—composers like Durante, Leo, Porpora, Jommelli, Galuppi, and Piccinni.

During the next century, the opera continued to revolve in the groove of the tradition established by Cavalli and Scarlatti. There were attempts to achieve a national style in countries outside of Italy: in France, this effort was made by Lully, also an Italian; in England, by Henry Lawes and Matthew Locke; in Austria, by Caldara and Fux; in Germany, by Heinrich Schütz and Reinhard Keiser. But though the opera occasionally experienced minor reforms in structure, and an occasional variety of style, the general form and content of the opera everywhere remained true to the standards set by the Italians.

And the abuses grew.

Further and further was the opera carried from the destiny planned for it by Monteverdi. The libretto became more and more incredible in subject matter, and

---

[1] Edward J. Dent, in *Alessandro Scarlatti*.

received increasingly absurd treatment. The situations were complicated beyond clarity; pageantry and pomp were given preference over genuine feeling. Now (with Lully) there was a ballet to assume excessive proportions and to impede the flow and direction of the drama. Now, too, the music had become little more than sheer adornment for a spectacle, adding little except sensuous pleasure. Now the stage had become the background for elaborate and cumbersome settings, and for grandiose stagecraft. Worst of all, now the writing for the voice had become more meretricious than ever, designed to exploit the remarkable virtuosity of the *castrato*.

For the *castrato*, or singing eunuch, was rapidly achieving the height of his fame throughout Europe, a fame which was not to decline until the end of the eighteenth century. These eunuchs, who were emasculated at an early age so that no change of voice might take place with puberty, were in great favor in opera and in church music. Their vocal range was equal to that of a female alto or soprano; but in power of voice and in its flexibility they far exceeded the technical equipment of even the greatest female singers. It was because of their elastic voices that opera composers were tempted to write arias so elaborately trimmed with runs, cadenzas and trills that frequently the melodies were hidden beyond detection behind the intricate embroidery.

As these abuses grew, the opera cried for a new reformer of the stature of Monteverdi. What was needed was a restoration of credibility, truth, forcefulness, feeling, simplicity; and simplicity above everything else.

In England there arose a free spirit who sensed what the true role of opera should be. In or about 1690, Henry Purcell was commissioned by a boarding school for girls in Chelsea to compose an opera. That opera, *Dido and Aeneas,* is "one of the most original expressions of genius in all opera," as one English musician spoke of it.[1]

The libretto of Nahum Tate is an ordinary one, occasionally dramatic in action, but more often employing verses of a discouragingly prosaic quality. Yet Purcell's genius gave the libretto wings and, through the music, the Tate lyrics—ordinary though they are—soared high. Purcell had an instinct which was infallible in its taste. That instinct forced him to abandon many of the abuses found in the other operas of the time. Only with Gluck is the ballet so integral a part of the action as it is with *Dido,* and only Monteverdi

[1] Gustav Holst, in *The Heritage of Music.*

[*49*]

before him and Gluck after him achieved such a wonderful fusion of music and text.

Most important is not that *Dido and Aeneas* is an opera through which beauty and feeling—both expressed unforgettably—course. More important is it that *Dido and Aeneas* follows the route of Monteverdi. For *Dido* is most poignant when it is simple and direct: the accompaniment to the famous lament of Dido, for example, is of an almost elementary structure—a simple ground bass for cellos and basses introduces the melody and serves as its background. *Dido* is most enchanting when it is unpretentious: the sunny-faced radiance of such choruses as *To the hills and the vales* and *Destruction's our delight* owe their charm to their simplicity and light hand of treatment. *Dido* is most dramatic when the music contributes color, suspense and atmosphere to the action on the stage: How tellingly the composer depicts through his music a storm (*The Grove*), the dark and mysterious movements of the Furies (*The Cave*), or the stir and movement of the harbor at a moment of the departure of a ship (*The Ships*).

No opera since Monteverdi and before Gluck achieved such vivid pictorial writing. Nor had any opera before Gluck expressed tragedy with such majesty and restraint, or—at other times—given voice to such a radiance of beauty. For Purcell had a gift that belonged to Monteverdi, a gift which Gluck was later to reveal. "He knew how to express human feelings in a language all divine."

Had the late seventeenth century had a clear understanding of the artistic mission of the opera, it is more than likely that a work so wonderfully integrated, so surely and completely realized as *Dido and Aeneas* would have exerted a powerful influence on composers everywhere. As it was, *Dido and Aeneas* stands alone and neglected among the operas of the time. There was then too little comprehension of true operatic principles for *Dido* to create a definite school, or to bring an issue into the open and resolve that issue into an inevitable struggle of principles.

Soon after the death of Purcell another reformer of the opera arose. He produced no work that deserves to stand with *Dido and Aeneas,* yet his influence was great, and it is largely to his experimentation that we owe the evolution of Gluck.

Jean Philippe Rameau was, like Monteverdi, an adventurer in tones. He had a sound understanding of the aesthetics of his art. First and foremost, he was a theoretician, and only secondly a composer. It has even been written that he looked somewhat contemptuously upon music as an imitative art which was based upon a routined system of harmony. He composed—so it was sometimes said of him—only to give practical application to his theories.

He theorized about harmony and became one of the first to formulate the science of modern harmony into extraordinary texts. He also theorized about opera. He was dissatisfied with the way opera was being written. He set for himself the thankless task of the reformer. Others might clutter their opera with pretty melodies; he—in search of true dramatic writing—would give greater significance to harmony and rhythm than to lyricism. Others might apotheosize the voice of the *castrato;* he would give greater attention to the orchestra. He would, in short, break with the Italian tradition and would create a French manner of writing operas in which dramatic values were as significant as the musical.

He knew the abuses to which the reformer is inevitably subjected. Polemics were written against him, condemning the sterility of his music, its complexity, its dullness, its pretensions. Jean Jacques Rousseau wrote in his *Lettres sur la musique française:*

The French airs are not airs at all, and the French recitative is not recitative. I conclude, therefore, that the French have not and cannot have music of their own; or if they have one, it will be so much the worse for them!

The musicians of the Opéra orchestra would jeer at the difficulty of Rameau's orchestrations by complaining that there was no time in which to sneeze. Grimm laughed derisively at Rameau's excessive use of the ballet:

The French opera has become a spectacle in which the only unhappiness or happiness of its characters consists in watching people dance around them.

Even mocking verses were circulated by word of mouth to discredit Rameau:

If the difficult is pretty,
What a great man is Rameau!
If, by chance, whate'er is witty
Must be simple, then I know
He is but a little man!

Yet there were those who knew that, for all his faults, he was a great and important composer. "This man will eclipse us all," the celebrated French musician, Campra, said of him. And Voltaire wrote: "Rameau has made of music a new art."

He was born in the city of Dijon, France, on October 23, 1683, the son of a competent but indigent organist. He was only a child when he was first taught music. At the age of seven he could already perform on the harpsichord. Yet, strange to report, Rameau's father could not recognize any talent in his son, and decided that he was not meant for music. Jean Philippe, therefore, was sent to the Jesuit College for academic training. There he was a pupil uninterested in studies other than music. And when he left college, it was not with that sound and comprehensive education which his father had planned for him.

He loved music passionately. He knew that he would not be happy in a career that did not embrace it. He yearned to travel in Italy, then the scene of much rich music-making. In 1701, he was sent there by his father —not for the sake of the music which could be heard there, but rather for the sake of its distance from Dijon which might terminate an undesirable attachment which young Rameau had formed for a widow. For a short period, Rameau wandered through the northern cities of Italy, earning his living by playing the organ in churches and by performing in town bands.

Rameau was disappointed in Italy, and its music did not appeal to him so strongly as he had believed it would. In a short time, he was back in France. He became an organist at Avignon, then filled a similar post in Clermont. At the same time, he began his first compositions.

After six years in Clermont, Rameau—stifled by the constricted musical life of a small town—went to Paris and settled in rue du Temple. For the next few years he knew intense poverty. But personal suffering did not impede his study of music. He was a pupil of Louis Marchand in organ, and theory he acquired by devouring every book on the subject which he could find.

When Rameau first came to prominence in Paris, it was not as a composer but as a theoretician. In 1723, he published his monumental *Nouveau système de musique théorique,* which (together with his later works in the same field) has since become the basis of the science of modern harmony. It is this work which brought Rameau to the attention of the foremost music patron in France, Monsieur Riche de la Pouplinière. La Pouplinière sponsored Rameau's career. He appointed him conductor of his private orchestra, commissioned him to write music for that orchestra, placed an organ at his disposal, and brought him into direct contact with the leading musicians and the best music of the period.

In 1733, Rameau met his first success as a composer with an opera *Hippolyte et Aricie*. That success was further augmented in 1737 with his masterpiece, *Castor et Pollux*.

Despite his growing fame, Rameau, almost from the beginning of his career as opera composer, became the subject of bitter controversies and feuds. Heated battles were fought in his name. With *Hippolyte et Aricie* he aroused the Lullists. Rameau may have adhered to some of the traditions established by Lully: particularly in his use of the ballet and in his weakness for elaborate and colorful ceremonials on the stage. But in other respects, Rameau departed sharply from his predecessor, principally in his comparative neglect of singable melodies for the sake of enriched harmony. And for this departure, the followers of Lully could not forgive him.

With his succeeding operas—*Dardanus, Zoroastre,* and others—Rameau aroused the opposition of admirers of Italian opera. As with each work he adhered more and more rigidly to his self-imposed principles, and departed more and more sharply from the accepted traditions of opera-writing, the hostility against him grew and became intensified. He had by now become one of the foremost composers in France—and had earned the recognition of royalty which honored him with a pension of two thousand francs a year and the honorary title of "Compositeur de la musique de chambre." But neither fame nor recognition proved adequate in protecting him from the attacks of his enemies.

If the truth must be told, the fight against Rameau was centered as much upon a lustily disliked personality, as upon a composer with original theories of music. He had an instinctive capacity for losing friends and making enemies. He was loud-voiced and harsh, his manners were awkward and undisciplined. Those who came into contact with him were often irritated, sometimes enraged, by what he did or said. For tact was not one of his virtues. He was severe in his judgments of people, hard and callous in dealing with them. His conversation was often touched with acid. Besides, it was known that he was avaricious, capable of driving a hard bargain where money was concerned. He loved money, spent as little of it as possible—even denying himself many necessary comforts. He was, finally, a victim of moods. More often than not he was somber and melancholy, fastidiously avoiding the society of people (who likewise made it a practice to avoid him), spending his hours either in work at home, or in long solitary walks in the country—his favorite diversion.

The climax of this hostility against Rameau was reached in 1752 with a musical war that is spoken of by the historian as the *guerre des bouffons*. On August 1, a group of itinerant Italian singers introduced Pergolesi's *La serva padrona*. It was a tumultuous success; at the same time it crystallized the opposition to Rameau. An entire cult (including Grimm, Diderot, D'Alembert and Rousseau) proclaimed Pergolesi's comic-opera as the only true musical art, and viciously condemned Rameau for his intricate technique and dull cerebralism. Those who sided with Rousseau upheld the Italian traditions of opera; those who were with Rameau proclaimed his operas as true French art. Many years later, this operatic battle of principles was once again to be fought vitriolically in Paris, when the Italian tradition was pitted against the theories of Gluck; and it is interesting to note that in this battle, it was on the side of Rameau's successor that Jean Jacques Rousseau was to fight. Unfortunately, Rameau did not live to see the decisive victory of his ideals, as it was finally achieved by Gluck. But he did live to see himself proclaimed the greatest (if also the most liberally despised) composer in France, and to discern an increasing tendency on the part of the more discriminating French musicians toward siding with him against the Italians.

Jean Philippe Rameau died on September 12, 1764. Even in death he remained in character: It was reported that while on his deathbed, as he listened to a priest intoning prayers for him, he stingingly reproved him for being out of tune!

Actually, though he fought to liberate opera from the abuses it suffered at the hands of the Italians, he did not succeed in achieving this liberation himself. He was a composer of striking individuality and power of invention. He had a felicitousness of musical expression which, at its best, resulted in music of great beauty and grandeur. There are few moments in French opera which are as compelling in their beauty as the wonderful air of Thelaïre or as affecting as the funeral music, both from *Castor et Pollux.*

He brought to the opera a sense for the dramatic, an understanding of orchestral writing and a strength and originality of style which had a purifying effect on the stuffy opera-writing of the eighteenth century. Yet he did not go far enough. In too many respects he remained enslaved to tradition—a victim of pageantry, of his love for ballet, of ornate theatrical display. To hear his masterpiece, *Castor et Pollux,* in the twentieth century—as this writer did in Paris some years back— is to hear an opera touched by moments of magic, but an opera, nevertheless, which is stilted and untrue to life.

The complete liberation of opera, however, was a task left waiting for another genius—a genius with the self-assurance, strength, vision, pioneer independence and native gifts of a Monteverdi. Such a genius was found in Vienna in the middle of the eighteenth century. His name was Gluck.

But that is another—and later—story.

§ 2

THE oratorio is opera in another dress, or rather —if a feeble pun is permitted—opera in undress. Like the opera, it is a musical setting of a dramatic text, but the text is of a sacred rather than secular nature. Like opera, it calls for soloists, chorus and orchestra. However, it departs from the operatic formula by appearing without benefit of scenery or costumes.

It might, therefore, be expected that the first oratorio, like the first opera, would be the brain child of the Florentine "camerata." But, though conceived by the Florentine intellectuals, the first oratorio had roots which reached deeper than the sixteenth century. Musical settings of episodes from the Old and the New Tèstaments were in vogue during the fourteenth and fifteenth centuries; and they, in turn, stemmed from medieval morality and miracle plays.

Towards the close of the sixteenth century, St. Filippo Neri, the founder of the Congregation of the

Oratorians (so-called because its members met in the oratory of the Santa Maria in Vallicella in Rome), recognized that musical settings of the *Bible* could be uniquely effective in educating and inspiring the younger members of this religious order. He, therefore, introduced these musical settings before and after each of his sermons during weekday services in his oratory, and assigned the musical direction to Giovanni Animuccia.

These musical settings were first known as *Laudi spirituali,* but after a short period they came to be known as "oratorios," deriving this name from the place in which they were performed. The *Laudi spirituali,* or oratorios, proved popular, and even after the death of St. Filippo Neri in 1595 their performances were continued uninterruptedly in the Santa Maria Oratory.

The first *Laudi spirituali*—such as *The Good Samaritan* or *The Prodigal Son*—were spoken of as oratorios; but they could hardly be considered oratorios in the modern acceptance of that term. They were not essentially dramatic, and their form and scope were limited. They were more in the nature of fragments than complete and unified dramatic presentations.

But at the home of Giovanni Bardi, where the opera

was born, the oratorio form as we know it today grew from the embryo of the *Laudi spirituali*. And the father of the oratorio was Emilio del Cavalieri.

Emilio del Cavalieri was born in Rome in or about 1550. At an early age he went to Florence where he was employed in the court of Ferdinand de' Medici. He soon associated himself with Giovanni Bardi and his group of intellectuals. According to the testimony of some members of the "camerata," it was Cavalieri who was the first among them to write music in the new monodic style. He was also among the first composers in musical history to employ the figured bass, the spine of early homophonic music. After some experimentation with the new style (with musical pastorals, or scenes, such as *Il Satiro* and *La disperazione di Fileno*) he brought the *Nuove musiche* to the sacred text, just as his friend Peri introduced the new style into the theatre for a secular subject. In doing this Cavalieri evolved the oratorio—with a work entitled *La rappresentazione dell' anima e del corpo,* verses by Laura Guidiccioni. *La rappresentazione* was first performed in the Santa Maria Oratory in February of 1600. It is generally believed that Cavalieri did not live to hear his masterpiece performed.

It is the first work which assumes for us the general

outlines of the later oratorio, and for this reason historians will point to it as the first in this form. It may well be spoken of as the direct ancestor of Handel's *Messiah.*

It was called by its composer a "spiritual opera." It was elaborate in scope, calling for soloists, chorus, two orchestras (one, large and hidden, for the *ritornelli;* the other, a smaller group, for the accompaniments). It even utilized costumes and ballet (both of which were soon to be discarded by the oratorio).

Like Peri's *Euridice,* Cavalieri's *La rappresentazione* holds but little interest for the present-day music lover. The book is a dull and pretentious allegory in which abstract ideas such as Life, Body, Soul, Pleasure, World, Time, and so on become principal characters. The music is just as stilted and lifeless. The solo numbers are all in declamatory style, with recitatives that are dull and stereotyped. The choruses are almost naïve in character. The architectonic design of the work as a whole is not always clearly defined. A variety of mood and color, a greater skill in the projection of the dramatic elements of the text, and a fresher and more imaginative use of lyricism—these qualities were sadly lacking in the first oratorio.

But the first oratorio has pioneer significance. It

definitely showed another, and greater, composer his direction. That composer was Giacomo Carissimi.

Little is known of him, except a few scattered biographical facts. He was born in Marino, a small town near Rome, in 1605. We know, too, that in his twentieth year he was organist at the Cathedral of Tivoli. It was here that he first received recognition as a musician. For four years he was choirmaster in Assisi. Then, in 1628, he went to Rome to serve as master of the chapel at St. Apollinare, a post he held until the end of his life.

This is about all we know—this, and that in Rome his musical life unfolded, producing a remarkable series of oratorios: *Lucifer, Job, The Last Judgment, Abraham and Isaac, David and Jonathan, Daniel, Ezekias, Jephtha*—works which brought solidity of structure to the oratorio. Of his inner life, of his personality, of his spiritual conflicts we are completely in the dark. We can only guess that if the man was as his music, he must have been warm-hearted, soft, tender, and of a sunny nature.

Carissimi died in Rome in 1674. The oratorio, as he developed it, was inherited by a group of gifted pupils. He may well be called the Monteverdi of the oratorio, for like Monteverdi he found an embryo form and nursed it to full and mature growth. But the similarity between these two composers does not end here. Carissimi possessed many of Monteverdi's specific qualities as a composer. He had Monteverdi's powerful feeling for drama, his extraordinary capacity to inject dramatic feeling into music, and like Monteverdi he paid flattering attention to his texts and permitted them to guide him in his composition. He had Monteverdi's genius for lyric writing, and even achieved (as he did in the *"Lamentation"* from *Jephtha*) a warmer, more tender and sweeter melody than that which could be found even in the greatest Monteverdi operas. He had Monteverdi's independence in the bold use of harmony and in his employment of the orchestra. Like Monteverdi, Carissimi knew how to write recitatives that were powerful and dynamic, avoiding the stilted and fingerworn patterns of his predecessors; "he deprived it [the recitative] in a great measure of the formal closes and cadences which it had in common with the airs of that time," as the eminent historian George Hogarth wrote, "and rendered it more articulate and expressive by adopting the accents and inflections of speech."

But he was not just another and later Monteverdi.

[66]

He had qualities distinctly his own: principally an ability to be new without completely discarding the old. The members of the "camerata," and their immediate successors, were so eager to evolve a new art-form that they impatiently brushed aside the old polyphonic art. They considered polyphony as a style that had completely outlived its usefulness. But Carissimi recognized that the rich expressiveness of polyphonic writing need not be completely abandoned. He realized that an ingenious marriage between the old style and the new might well yield healthy offspring. Thus he supplemented his use of aria and recitative with choruses which leaned for support on the older style. Without abandoning counterpoint completely, he brought to choral writing the greater resources of harmony. He achieved, therefore, clear choral writing of a diaphanous transparency which the older polyphonists never fully realized. And he made his choral writing a supple means for descriptive writing.

In the field of the oratorio, Carissimi stands as the first of its masters; and all those who composed oratorios after his time were strengthened, guided, and enriched by his examples. The greatest composers of oratorio music have known and admired Carissimi, and have received direction from him—Alessandro

Scarlatti, for example. Even Handel was profoundly influenced by the Italian master. It is well known that Handel studied Carissimi and spoke highly of him. As a matter of fact, Handel once paid Carissimi the highest tribute of all—that of imitation: for a passage from Handel's *Samson* is unmistakably derived from a chorus in Carissimi's *Jephtha*.

It should be added, parenthetically, that together with the oratorio, Carissimi evolved the church cantata, a form of sacred music smaller in scope than the oratorio, and more intimate, suitable for performance in a chamber or small concert room. Carissimi conceived the church cantata only because he knew that there were churches which did not have the adequate facilities with which to present works of so elaborate a nature as his oratorios. He, therefore, created a new form, more intimate in quality and less pretentious in scope—a form which could be conveniently used for sacred works and which might be performed even with the most limited resources. Once again Carissimi struck important pioneer ground; for the church cantata was soon to be developed into extraordinary artistic dimensions by Buxtehude, and especially by Johann Sebastian Bach.

EARLY OPERA AND ORATORIO

The successors of Carissimi were many, and in the further evolution of the oratorio they performed no negligible roles. Among the immediate Italian followers of Carissimi were Stradella and, as said before, Alessandro Scarlatti.

No doubt Stradella's picaresque life-story is more famous than his music, for his strange romance has been told in legend, fiction and even in opera. But it is of greater importance, if not of greater interest, to remark that Stradella was the composer of a masterpiece than that he was the protagonist in a turbulent and ultimately tragic love affair. Stradella's most famous work is an oratorio, *San Giovanni Battista,* a work rich in melodic ideas and skillful in their treatment. "The recitative is in general excellent," wrote Burney, "and there is scarce a movement among the airs in which genius, skill, and study do not appear."

But the greater composer, no doubt, is that incomparable Neapolitan, Alessandro Scarlatti, whose influence in music was felt in so many different directions. Stradella was the composer of a masterpiece; but it was Scarlatti who was the successor to Carissimi. Numerous are the oratorios of Scarlatti! With his inexhaustible genius for aria writing, Scarlatti brought altogether new beauty to the solo sections of his works. And his skillful sense of form brought resilience to the design of the oratorio, making it more adaptable than ever before for a variety of colors, moods, and sentiments.

One historian [1] has admirably summarized Scarlatti's far-reaching contributions to the oratorio:

> With Scarlatti, the severe harsh outline of the forms used by the old canonical contrapuntists was softened by a free, graceful melody. It was greatly to his advantage that he employed the old church style, because in it he had, ready made, a form impregnated with deep religious earnestness. In place of the old strict thematic counterpoint, he substituted a freer development of parts so musically worked out that the result was the growth of a new and vigorous church style which rapidly gained adherents among musicians and was soon also to win the favor of the people.

Great though was the contribution of Alessandro Scarlatti to it, the oratorio required further preparation before it arrived at its ultimate stage of artistic growth with Bach and Handel. That final preparation

[1] Emil Naumann, in *The History of Music*.

it now received from a German master—one of the first of the great German composers in musical history —Heinrich Schütz.

Heinrich Schütz was born in Köstritz, Saxony, on October 8, 1585. His beautiful voice during his boyhood drew the admiration of the Landgraf Maurice of Hesse-Cassel. The Landgraf urged Schütz's parents to entrust the boy to him for his musical and academic training.

In 1599, Schütz became chorister at the chapel of the Landgraf. At the same time he was enrolled in a school devoted to children of nobility. When he completed his education here, Schütz was enrolled in the University of Marburg for the study of law.

Schütz's pronounced musical gifts convinced the Landgraf that the young man should specialize in the art. In 1609, Schütz was permitted to leave the university and to travel to Italy to study with Giovanni Gabrieli. He now came into contact for the first time with the *Nuove musiche,* which later he was to adapt to the German temperament and language in his greater choral works. In Italy, Schütz published his first work, a book of songs—his first attempt at writing in the new vein.

When, in 1612, Gabrieli died, Schütz returned to

Germany to serve as organist for the Landgraf. Two years later, the Elector of Saxony heard Schütz direct a performance and was determined to have this remarkable musician as his Kapellmeister in Dresden. He pleaded and argued with the Landgraf, and finally convinced him, to part with his protégé.

Heinrich Schütz served as Kapellmeister in Dresden until the end of his life. He reorganized the music of the chapel along Italian lines, even importing special instrumentalists from Italy. For fifty-seven years, he dominated the musical life of Dresden and brought to it an importance unparalleled in Saxony at the time. He was given periodic vacations from his musical duties. In 1628, he visited Italy a second time. Now he came into contact with the music of Monteverdi and Carissimi, and was profoundly influenced by it. In 1633—during the Thirty Years' War—he left the Dresden chapel on three different occasions to become Kapellmeister in Copenhagen, but he was back permanently in his original post in Dresden in 1645, and now held the position without interruption until his death. Like Beethoven, Schütz knew during the last years of his life the greatest curse that can fall upon a composer: deafness. And like Beethoven he transformed a curse into a blessing. It helped him to bring to his music a spirituality and other-worldliness which is so often found in the last quartets of Beethoven.

Heinrich Schütz died in Dresden on November 6, 1672. A contemporary who was with Schütz at the time of his death has left us the following account of the composer's last hours:

> On the sixth of November . . . he arose . . . and dressed; and after nine o'clock, while he was searching for something in his room, he was seized by a sudden weakness and he was stricken by apoplexy. . . . The doctor, who had been called without delay, applied all his care to succor him with excellent remedies . . . but there was nothing that could help him. At the same time, the spiritual father was called to his side. . . . He blessed him, and almost immediately, he [Schütz] rested very tranquil. . . . And when the fourth hour struck, he died quietly and peacefully, without the least convulsion, while we, at his side, were praying and singing.

Heinrich Schütz represents the transition from Carissimi and Scarlatti to Handel and Bach. In the history of the oratorio, he is the connecting link between its era of earliest development and its period of greatest fruition. Schütz's oratorios—together with his oratorio-Passions (which were more specific applications of the Gospel story of the passion of Christ, and the direct predecessors of Bach's Passions)—are richer in harmonic inventiveness than the works of the Italians, even if they are also less lyrical. With Schütz thought is frequently given precedence over emotion, feeling gives way to contemplation. For the free-flowing, incandescent melodies of Carissimi, and the wonderfully singable arias of Scarlatti, Schütz substituted an intensified drama—even to the point of using program music. Schütz's music, however, has, at certain moments, a spiritual quality; it is sublime and introspective. At such moments, he makes us think of the holier pages in Bach's Passions.

Heinrich Schütz died thirteen years before Johann Sebastian Bach and Handel were born. Schütz had been born into an older period of the oratorio, but died before the dawn of the new. New ages are born because there were great men to dream of them, and to work to achieve them. The new age of the oratorio— the age of Bach and Handel—was made possible because Heinrich Schütz had worked for it. In the history of German music, as well as in the history of the oratorio, his figure looms large. He was the first of that magisterial line of German composers which extended through Bach and Handel, through Beethoven and Schumann, to Wagner and Richard Strauss.

§ 3

THE oratorio arrived at full maturity somewhat sooner than did the opera. Not until a decade or so after the death of Bach did the opera achieve that aesthetic mission which had first been conceived for it by Monteverdi. It realized this with Gluck. Gluck is not only one of the greatest of the early reformers of the opera. More than that, he must be ranked with Monteverdi, Wagner, and Debussy as one of its most significant influences. One brings to mind the operas heard in Gluck's time. In comparing them with *Orfeo ed Euridice* (once again is Orpheus called upon to liberate opera with his lute!) one begins to realize the full extent of the liberation achieved by opera. Artificial texts, cluttered with impossible situations, received from composers an equally artificial musical treatment. The more ornamental the melodic line, the better it revealed the vocal dexterity of the *castrato;* for it was the art of the *castrato,* and not the art of the composer, that assumed first significance with the opera audi-

[*76*]

ences of the seventeenth and early eighteenth centuries. In the writing of these decorative melodies, Sammartini, Caldara, Porpora, Leo, Reinhard Keiser, Hasse were as masterful as the Viennese court-poet Metastasio (the favored librettist of the age) was in the fashioning of euphuistic flowers of speech. These composers felt that music was to please the ear and lull the senses. To have it serve as an integral, even indispensable, part of the artistic whole of the opera was not to be thought of.

Rarely was there in the operatic music of the time a sincerely felt sentiment, rarely a profound emotion, simply and unpretentiously expressed. True there was often to be found an outpouring of lyric beauty. But this lyricism was too often divorced from and unrelated to the text.

There were exceptions, few and far between, which might have brought to Gluck his first recognition of the role opera could really perform: not only Purcell and Rameau, but even an opera like Handel's *Rinaldo*. But these were lonely exceptions in the operatic writing of the period preceding and contemporary with Gluck. They hardly deprive the Bohemian-born master of his right to be considered the father of the music-drama.

He knew what he was doing. He saw his direction with amazing clarity of vision. He never seemed to lack the conviction and self-assurance that the road he finally selected to unexplored territories was the only right road for the opera. With no precedent to guide him (unless Monteverdi's early attempts in this direction be called a precedent), he marched with amazingly little digression straight toward his goal. He accepted some of the less desirable opera conventions of his time —the aria form, for example, and the use of the ornamental ballet; but what he accepted, he revivified and made integral parts of his artistic scheme.

He was dissatisfied with the libretto of the day; what he wanted was a text that was true to human experiences, real and natural, with characters who were something more than marble statues of historic figures. The flowered decorations of the opera aria of the time irritated him; what he sought in music was a "noble simplicity." He groped for a more intimate relationship between text and music, the one supplementing the other, the one giving the other deeper and subtler shades of meaning. He sought to dramatize orchestral accompaniments. He wanted to subordinate the role of the singer, to make his art the servant of the music

[*78*]

and not its master. He aspired to integrate every element of the opera, even the often superfluous ballets, into an artistic unity. And in striving for these things, he was Monteverdi's successor and the precursor of Richard Wagner.

Read his own words! They are spoken by a man who knew what he was about.

> When one wishes to keep to the truth, one's style must be adapted to the subject that is being treated. The greatest beauties of melody and harmony become imperfections when they are out of place in the whole.

Or again:

> I do not by any means believe that you would gain pleasure in hearing a beautiful piece of music. I assure you, on the contrary, that you would have lost by it. For a beauty in the wrong place has not only the disadvantage of losing a great part of its effect but also of injuring the whole by leading the spectator astray, who then does not so easily find himself in a fitting position to follow with interest the course of the music drama.

Or even this:

> Before I work, I try above everything else to
> forget that I am a musician. I forget myself in
> order to see only my characters.

Or, best of all, his remarkable preface to his opera,
Alceste, in which once and for all he formulated his
theories on opera clearly and unequivocally:

> I endeavored to restrict music to its proper
> function, that of seconding the poetry by en-
> forcing the expression of the sentiment and the
> interest of the situations without interrupting
> the action or weakening it by superfluous orna-
> ment. . . . I have been careful never to inter-
> rupt a singer in the heat of the dialogue in or-
> der to introduce a tedious *ritornello,* nor to stop
> him in the middle of a word for the purpose of
> displaying the flexibility of his voice on some
> favorable vowel. . . . I have also thought that
> my chief endeavor should be to attain a grand
> simplicity, and consequently I have avoided
> making a parade of difficulties at the cost of
> clearness; I have set no value on novelty as such,
> unless it was naturally suggested by the situa-

tion and suited to the expression. In short, there was no rule which I did not consider myself bound to sacrifice for the sake of effect.

Words such as these announce the birth of the music-drama.

The birth of the music-drama might well be said to have taken place in Vienna on October 5, 1762. For it was then, at the famous Burgtheater, that Gluck's *Orfeo ed Euridice* was introduced.

Christoph Willibald Gluck came to Vienna in 1736, a broad-shouldered, heavy-set young man of twenty-two, of peasant stock. He had been born in Bohemia on July 4, 1714, and his first schooling had taken place in the Catholic schools where his training included instruction on the violin and violoncello. Later, at the Jesuit school in Komotau, he was taught the organ and the piano. When he was eighteen years old, he set off for Prague. Then, for the next few years, he led the life of a wandering minstrel, sustaining himself by singing in church choirs and by playing the violin at village fairs. He had been encouraged by the nobleman, Ferdinand Philip Lobkowitz (on whose father's estate his own father had been a forester) to come to Vienna. In Vienna, Prince Lobkowitz took young

Gluck under his wing, gave him employment in his intensely musical household, brought him into contact with the music and the musicians of the day, and encouraged him in his musical growth.

At the Lobkowitz palace, Gluck met Prince Melzi who, impressed by the young musician's gifts, offered to take him to Italy for further study. In Italy, Gluck studied with the master, Sammartini. The fruits of this study were Gluck's first operas, written in the traditional style of the Italian masters. From Italy, Gluck traveled to England, France, Leipzig, Dresden. Then, following a short visit to Bohemia to attend the bed of his dying father, he returned to Vienna. He had been gone from the Austrian capital twelve years, and in that time he had grown in self-assurance, skill and experience.

The year of his return to Vienna was 1748. On May 14 of that year his first opera to be produced in Vienna, *Semiramide riconosciuta,* reopened the Burgtheater. *Semiramide* was hardly a warning of the direction Gluck was to take in later years. Its text was by Metastasio—with that elaborateness of plot, overdecoration of poetic speech, unreality of situations and characters which marked so many of Metastasio's librettos. And Gluck followed the teachings of the Italian masters

[*82*]

diligently. The arias exploited the full resources of the singers. The accompaniments were, for the most part, formalistic. Infrequently, the influence of Rameau (whose operas Gluck had heard in Paris) asserted itself despite the dictates of Italian tradition—particularly in the dramatic feeling of some of the recitatives and in the nobility of one or two arias, such as the *"Tradita sprezzata"* and *"Che quel cor."* But for the most part Gluck was speaking in the language best understood and most highly appreciated by the Italian-loving Viennese nobility. His opera pleased Empress Maria Theresa, and delighted the music lovers of the city. It brought his name to the forefront of the composers in Vienna at the time.

The success of *Semiramide* notwithstanding, Gluck left Vienna for further travel (inspired to do so, perhaps, by the dangerous and disconcerting success of the visiting Italian, Niccolò Jommelli). But in 1750 he returned to Vienna to marry Marianne Pergin. He now settled permanently in Vienna and proceeded to solidify his position as composer. This was not slow in taking place. The Empress favored him more than once. In 1754, she recommended him for appointment as chief of the court orchestra at an annual salary of two thousand gulden.

Gluck, increasingly dissatisfied with the old established formulas of opera, as propounded by the all-
powerful Metastasio, and ever in impatient search of a
brave new world, was soon to find two powerful allies
in Vienna. It was their influence and far-sightedness,
almost as much as Gluck's own genius, which were responsible for *Orfeo*. One of these two was Count Giacomo Durazzo, assistant to Count Esterházy as director
of the court theatres. Durazzo came to Vienna in 1732,
then thirty years of age. Of gifted presence, and brilliant
of mind, he was a true dilettante, with a profound love
for music and the theatre. His tastes bent towards
French ideas and French culture; it was his aim to insti-
tute French reforms in the Italianate Burgtheater. With
him, in this aim, was the adventurer Ranieri de' Calsabigi, gambler, lover, literary genius, *bel esprit,* friend
of Casanova. Calsabigi came to Vienna in 1761, fresh
from Paris, bringing with him enthusiasm for the intellectual revolution which was then sweeping through
England and France at the time and was soon to engulf
all of Europe, a revolution which spoke in the names
of simplicity, humanity, naturalness, and whose spokes-
men were Rousseau, Diderot, and Voltaire.

Simplicity, humanity, naturalness; they were to a
degree found in the operas of Rameau which Gluck

[*84*]

had learned to admire long since. Thus, inevitably, three spirits, all of whom had been inspired by French examples, moved closer to one another: Durazzo, Calsabigi, and Gluck. They soon discovered each other's profound sympathy for a new type of opera, an opera which would bridge the gap between the artificiality of the Italians and the cerebralism of the French; an opera which—following the example of the French—would restore to the stage dignity, simplicity, and the moving emotion of the Greek tragedy. "I thought that here was the secret of writing excellent music to a drama," wrote Calsabigi many years later, in recalling his early aims and ideals, "that the more compact, energetic, passionately touching, harmonious the poetry was, the more would the music that should express it thoroughly, in accordance with its true declamation, be the genuine music of that poetry, music *par excellence*." Away with the Italian manners of opera writing as glorified by the Metastasio libretto, with their superficial veneer, trite ornaments, and lack of any deep conviction and true feeling!

Thus an undeclared artistic war was soon waged in Vienna. On the one side were the three proponents of French art. On the other, the ruling figure of the old Italian school—Metastasio, and with him the many composers who thought as he did and were inspired by his dramas. As Calsabigi later wrote:

> Everyone in Vienna knows that the imperial poet, Metastasio, belittled Gluck, and that the feeling was mutual. For Gluck thought little of Metastasio's meticulous drama. He was of the opinion that this high-flown poetry and these neatly manufactured characters had nothing that was great and elevated to offer to music. . . . Gluck hated those meek political, philosophical and moral views of Metastasio, his metaphors, his garrulous little passions, his geometrically devised word-plays. Gluck liked emotion captured from simple nature. . . . The imperial poet, on the other hand, took delight in ingenious flowers of speech, which he liked to present in the form of antitheses, in amorous disputes, in academic discourses, in petty characters one and all of lovelorn affectations. The minds of these two were diametrically opposed to each other.

It was out of this war that the music-drama emerged, inspired by French models. But in the completeness of its form and expression it went far beyond anything conceived by Rameau.

Gluck had come from peasant stock; he remained something of a peasant to the end of his days. He had the hardness of flesh and hardihood that are cultivated from working the soil. He looked the peasant—and acted like one. He was large of bone, heavy-set; his jaw was square; his cheek-bones, high; his complexion, ruddy. He had large peasant hands, and eyes that were direct and far-seeing.

His behavior coördinated well with his appearance. Not even years of constant intimacy with the high-born of Vienna and Paris could rid him of his peasant traits. He was almost boorish in his manners. He spoke in a loud voice, and he was not always careful of what he was saying. He was sometimes coarse, and always ill-poised. In the society of people, he was usually stiff and uncomfortable; for, truth to tell, he did not like people very much. What he liked was money, the good things of life, his wife, his niece, the comradeship of a handful of intimate friends; and he liked best his own music.

He was self-confident almost to a point of arrogance.

Convinced of his own destiny as a composer, he did not hesitate to speak rhapsodically of his own works, and almost with an objectivity as if they were the works of another composer. And yet he disliked flattery, and grew irritable and hot-tempered when he felt he was being catered to. He was fiercely proud. He was also stubborn. This stubbornness, this pride, this self-assurance, this faith in his destiny were what gave him that remarkable singleness of purpose which characterized his artistic career. Not feuds nor enmities, however bitter; not crushing defeats nor personal humiliations could divert him from his direction.

The first shot fired in the operatic war in Vienna was a ballet called *Don Juan* presented at the Burgtheater on October 17, 1761. The scenario was based on Molière's *Le festin de pierre,* and the French text was prepared by Calsabigi; the music was by Gluck. Durazzo's dream of a French art supplanting the Italian at the Burgtheater was on its way to realization. But Durazzo knew (and undoubtedly Calsabigi and Gluck as well) that a bolder thrust than *Don Juan* was needed in order to overthrow the reign of Metastasio. What was needed was an opera based completely on the new principles they had discussed and formulated.

And so, *Orfeo* was conceived. . . .

With Durazzo's encouragement and advice, Calsa-bigi prepared a libretto that was strong but simple, with characters drawn from Greek mythology who were not of plaster or clay but of flesh and blood, warm with human feelings, pulsing with emotion. Gluck was called upon to prepare music in the spirit of such a text.

The contemporary Zinzendorf recorded how, in July of 1762, the *castrato* Guadagni sang parts from *Orfeo* at Calsabigi's home on the Kohlmarkt before a distinguished audience of friends. Rehearsals soon be-gan in earnest, marked by the indefatigable severity of the composer who knew what he wanted and was dis-satisfied with anything less than the complete realiza-tion of his wishes.

Finally, on October 5, 1762, the first performance of *Orfeo* took place at the Burgtheater. The audience included the élite of Viennese society: the Empress Maria Theresa, the Duke of Braganza, Prince and Princess Esterházy, Prince Kaunitz, and many others. And as the simple but eloquent story of Orpheus un-folded with directness and force—the music as strong and as unpretentious as the text—musical history was in the making; though it is certain that few in that

glittering audience that night were even faintly aware
of this fact.

To that audience, *Orfeo* was, for the most part, a
disappointment. Gluck was the foremost composer in
Vienna at the time, and the audience had come expecting much. The plot of the libretto seemed devoid of
any action—a threadbare text: Only three characters
in all (with the chorus acting as a fourth), moving in a
plot of almost elementary simplicity! The music appeared hardly more gracious. One or two arias had
pleasing melodies, and to these the audience reacted
warmly. But the other arias, denuded as they were of
long, intricate runs and decorative *fioriture,* seemed
stark. The piercing cacophonies of the Hades scene
seemed to those eighteenth century ears as more noise
than drama; the orchestra seemed turgid (who ever
heard of kettledrums, cymbals and trombones in an
orchestra?).

The ears that heard *Orfeo* for the first time were
deaf to its many wonders. They failed to perceive the
wonderful adjustment of words to melody, of action
to musical sound—suited to each other, emphasizing
and underscoring each other, giving each other new
penetrating meaning. It failed to understand that the

[*90*]

tone-painting—from the gruesome horrors of the un-
derworld to the seraphic beatitude of Elysium—was
achieved with an amazing economy. The chorus and
the ballet were now integral parts of the drama. And
through simplicity and deep feeling, the music
achieved a poignancy of sentiment which other composers of the Italian tradition could not suggest with
all their artifice and skill. "There is no other opera in
the world's long list," as Henry Chorley wrote many
years later, "which, with merely three female voices
and a chorus, can return to the stage in days like ours to
make the heart throb and the eyes water."

But it cannot be said that with the first performance
of *Orfeo* the reign of Metastasio came to an end in
Vienna. For *Orfeo* was a failure—it was not to be successful for another two years. It was a human drama,
and not a spectacle for the eye and an opiate for the
senses; and this, the eighteenth century Viennese nobility were not prepared to accept immediately. Yet
Orfeo marked a sharp divergence of the opera-form
from the Italians towards a new horizon; and that new
horizon was *Tristan und Isolde*.

But Gluck was not to stand still. After *Orfeo* came
Alceste in which the experiments continued boldly

and, in certain moments, went even beyond its predecessor. An overture no longer prefaced the new opera,
for an overture was often an ornamental superfluity;
to *Alceste,* Gluck prefixed an *intrada,* an introduction
which with the first mighty descending chords set the
tone, the mood, the character of the play that was to
follow. And there were pages in *Alceste* in which the
music-drama reached high moments of realization, and
none more moving or more dramatic than the *Chorus
of Spirits* (consisting entirely of the repeated "F"—an
amazing adventure in simplicity and dramatic force),
or the justly famous *Divinités du Styx* with its astute
changes of tempo and color.

Alceste was not successful. The far-seeing (and they
were few) recognized its greatness. Sonnenfels spoke
rapturously about an opera which could be a "serious
work without men-sopranos, music without solfeggios,
or, as I might rather say, without squealing, an Italian
poem without turgidity and nonsense." But the public
thought *Alceste* a bore. One characteristic contemporary remark was that only a game of chess could fill in
"the void in these long recitatives."

The opera which followed *Alceste, Paride ed Elena,*
was an even greater failure. Gluck momentarily knew
the bitterness of defeat.

Only in the hope that I might find imitators did I publish the music of *Alceste,* and I flattered myself that the others would be eager to follow the road I had broken for them, in order to destroy the evil practices which have crept into the Italian opera and have dishonored it. I am now convinced that my hopes were in vain. The half-learned, the judges and legislators of art—a class of persons unfortunately too numerous, and at the same time of greater disadvantage to art than ignoramuses—rage against a method which, if established, would obviously endanger their criteria.

But his faith in the new world he had discovered was unshaken, and he remained stubborn and resolute in his purpose.

No obstacles shall deter me from making new attempts to achieve my purpose. *Sufficit mihi unus Plato per cuncto populo;* [I would rather have one Plato on my side than all the populace].

But he felt that he would have to leave Vienna. Durazzo had already departed a few years earlier, a victim of court intrigues. Calsabigi, too, had been forced to leave—also under a cloud. Gluck now felt that he was fighting the battle alone.

He preferred to find a new scene for the struggle, and, perhaps, a more amenable audience. He was thinking specifically of Paris, where Rameau had first inspired him with a new mission. And from Paris, his one-time pupil, Marie Antoinette, was repeatedly sending him invitations.

In 1773, Gluck left Vienna. In Paris, the operatic war, which had begun in the Austrian capital, was to be brought to its successful culmination.

In Vienna, Gluck had fought against Metastasio. In Paris, it was Niccola Piccinni who was the spearhead of the opposition.

Gluck arrived in Paris in the fall of 1773. On April 18th of the following year, his first French opera— *Iphigénie en Aulide*—was produced. Things did not go smoothly for Gluck. The singers he found incompetent, and the orchestra, he said, was like "an old coach drawn by consumptive horses, and led by one deaf from birth." Everywhere, Gluck met antagonism and envy. There were the old bouffonists who still glorified the Italian traditions and still looked upon Pergolesi as the model for all operatic writing—and among them was Jean Jacques Rousseau, soon to become Gluck's staunchest advocate. There were also those who would not receive a foreigner into the *Académie de la musique*. In every direction, Gluck found opposition, enmity, and the demand for impossible concessions. The dancer Vestris, for example, insisted upon a *chaconne* for the end of the opera. ("Who ever heard of Greeks dancing a *chaconne?*" pathetically asked Gluck. "Well, if they did not," answered Vestris sharply, "it is so much the worse for them!") But for the personal intervention of Marie Antoinette herself, the opera might have never obtained performance.

Yet, once performed, the opera gripped Paris. The overture was encored, and some of the scenes so moved the audience that its enthusiasm was expressed with boisterous approval. "At last, a great triumph!" wrote Marie Antoinette. "On the nineteenth, we had the first performance of Gluck's *Iphigénie*. I was carried away by it. We can find nothing else to talk about. You can scarcely imagine what excitement reigns in all minds in regard to this event. It is incredible." The opera became a principal subject for salon conversation. Each night the receipts of the Opéra exceeded five thousand livres—an unheard-of figure. So popular grew the opera that the ladies of Paris went so far as to adopt a hair-dress which they called *à l'Iphigénie!*

Iphigénie was followed by an even more successful presentation of *Orfeo* in August of 1775. Gluck's popularity was greatly solidified by *Orfeo,* and the ranks of those who sympathized with his aims swelled: they now included Voltaire, Bailli du Rolet, Corancez, Mlle Lespinasse and the Abbé Arnaud—powerful figures all.

But the enemies were equally strong.

Shortly after Gluck had been commissioned to prepare an opera to a text by Quinault, *Roland,* the enemies succeeded in inducing Marie Antoinette to bring to Paris the famous Italian composer, Niccola Piccinni, to prepare an Italian opera on the same libretto. The news of this treachery reached Gluck while he was absent from Paris. It so infuriated him that he destroyed his own opera and despatched a fiery letter to *L'Année littéraire.* That letter sounded the call to battle. Two distinct camps once again appeared in Paris. At the head of one was Marmontel, who found Gluck's music to be full of "harsh and rugged harmony, incoherent modulations and incongruities, mutilations, and so forth." On the other side was Jean Jacques Rousseau (a deserter from the camp of the bouffonists)—who now wrote: "Gluck alone appears to set himself the aim of giving to each of the personages the style that is proper to him."

The struggle was no less bitter than it had been in Vienna. "Women and men alike entered the fray," the Baroness Oberkirch reported. "Such passion and fury were roused that people had to be separated. Many friends and even lovers quarreled on this account." "They are tearing each other's eyes out here, for or against Gluck," wrote Mme Riccoboni to David Garrick. Marmontel, La Harpe, D'Alembert, Coqueau, and many others attacked Gluck vitriolically (Marmontel even wrote a long poem in praise of Italian opera and Piccinni). Rousseau, Suard, and Abbé Arnaud spoke for Gluck.

When *Alceste* was produced in Paris, and without success, it seemed that victory belonged to the Italian. But the culminating battle was soon at hand. The shrewd director of the Opéra, realizing that rivalries such as that of Gluck and Piccinni were profitable for the box-office, commissioned both composers to prepare the music for a text entitled *Iphigénie en Tauride*. One composer was to write in his own new style, while the other was to follow the Italian tradition.

On March 18, 1778, Gluck's opera was produced; it

was to be followed somewhat later by Piccinni's work. The triumph that met Gluck's opera was unmistakable. "I know not if what we have heard is melody," wrote Melchior Grimm after the first performance. "Perhaps it is something much better. I forget the opera, and find myself in a Greek tragedy."

Disconcerted by Gluck's success, Piccinni attempted to withdraw his own opera from production. But the director refused to release him from his contract. The performance of Piccinni's opera was a fiasco, as everyone expected it would be.

There could no longer exist any doubt as to which side had won the decisive victory. In June of 1781, the *Mercure de France* summed up Gluck's personal triumph, and the triumph of the music-drama over the Italian opera, when it wrote: "The works of Gluck are about the only fortune of operatic music."

The operatic war ended. The music-drama was victorious in spite of enmity, cabals, and opposition. Gluck returned to Vienna there to spend the last years of his life. His right to be called one of the masters of music was no longer questioned. The great of the earth came to his little home in Perchtoldsdorf to pay him homage. There he died on the fifteenth of November, 1787.

His achievement [as one modern critic [1] wrote] consists in the fact that he thrust the doors open and allowed the daylight of human naturalness to fall upon the opera world of the time. In that light it was natural that many things should assume an aspect different from that which they had had under the half-light of the eunuch atmosphere that had hitherto obtained. Artistic virtuosity for its own sake gave way to a newly crystallizing purity of song. Reason and logic asserted their rights as men began to sing with their natural voices. Intellect and feeling of a clear and purified attitude toward art arose to form a critical conscience, which tested the art work for its possibilities in the light of the demands of a new ideal of form.

[1] Paul Bekker, in *The Changing Opera.*

§ 4

THERE was more than one manner of reacting against the artificiality of the stylized Italian opera of the seventeenth and early eighteenth centuries. One method was that of Gluck in his creation of the first music-drama. But a completely different reaction (and no less successful in its own right) could be found in the opera buffa of Pergolesi. That Pergolesi's opera buffa was used as the spearhead with which to attack first Rameau and then Gluck himself does not in any way make it less revolutionary in its attempt to depart from the formal and stilted Italian patterns of opera writing.

The opera buffa reacted against the stiff historic or classical figures who stalked the stage of the Italian opera. The opera buffa, therefore, called upon characters who were everyday human beings: scheming servants, cuckolds, deceived wives. The opera buffa was as dissatisfied as the music-drama with the artificial, ornamented arias which were created only to exploit flexible voices; it therefore used simple tunes, of a highly melodious nature, but chiseled down in design to their barest essentials, tunes capable of catching the fancy of an audience with a first hearing. The complicated and often indecipherable plots of remote interest that dominated the librettos of serious Italian operas were supplanted in the opera buffa by farcical stories of popular interest; and these stories were told with the greatest possible economy, using situations sparingly and calling upon only a limited number of characters.

Long before Pergolesi composed his first opera buffa, the use of comic characters in brief comic scenes (these scenes were called *intermezzi*) had been part and parcel of Italian operatic writing. These comic scenes were an outgrowth of the traditional *commedia dell' arte,* and were adopted by the Neapolitan composers within the formal framework of the opera. With Alessandro Scarlatti, these *intermezzi* received such importance of treatment, and were so lustily appreciated by the audiences, that the historian is often tempted to speak of Scarlatti as the important transition from the opera seria to the opera buffa.

In 1709, an intimate theatre was opened in Naples devoted exclusively to the presentation of little musical farces of which the librettos were written in native dialect. For this theatre, Alessandro Scarlatti wrote a successful score in 1718. It was not long before younger composers began to write for this new theatre. One of these was Nicola Logroscino (1698–1765), who wrote several popular operas in the comic vein. Logroscino is believed to have been the first composer to employ the *finale,* a favorite device of all later comic operas for the closing of each act, and one of the contributions of the opera buffa to serious operatic writing. But Logroscino seems to have had limited creative gifts. He had a flair for the popular, and his tunes had peasant lustiness. But he had no clear conception of the potentialities of the opera buffa form. His works were little more than comedies generously interspersed with popular tunes. Of unity of purpose or of coherence in design there seems to have been little.

It was with Pergolesi that the opera buffa emerged full-grown for the first time. In Pergolesi, as in Gluck, musical history possessed one of those rare creative spirits whose work not only blazed significant pioneer trails, but also whose work has remained fresh to the present time. Pergolesi may not rank, as Gluck most assuredly does, with those giants in music who fashioned complete and magnificent worlds. His was a smaller world of beauty; but it was no less perfect. We do not condemn a meadow for not being an Alpine peak; and it would be ridiculous to condemn Pergolesi's opera buffa because it was no Gluck's *Orfeo.* In the Valhalla of great composers, Pergolesi may not have been one of the gods; but among the demi-gods his position is surely of no little significance.

Giovanni Battista Pergolesi was born in Jesi, near Ancona, on January 4, 1710. He was the son of a surveyor. His earliest instruction in music took place on the violin under Francesco Santini, then under Francesco Mondini. In his sixteenth year, Pergolesi acquired the patronage of Count Cardolo Maria Manelli who entered him in the Conservatory in Naples. There Pergolesi's teachers included some of the most eminent masters of the time, including Gaetano Greco, Francesco Durante and Francesco Feo.

Pergolesi composed his first large work in 1731. It was a sacred drama entitled *La conversione di San Guglielmo d'Aquitania* which, it is significant to note, contained a diverting intermezzo. The performance of this work at the Saint Agnello Maggiore monastery was sufficiently successful to bring its composer a commission from the court theatre in Naples for a second opera. *La Sallustia,* the work that had been commissioned, likewise contained a comic intermezzo, as did its successor, *Ricimero*.

Thus, having somewhat timidly tried his wings three times as a composer of comic interludes, Pergolesi was now prepared for his first full flight.

In 1733, Pergolesi composed *La serva padrona,* his first opera entirely in the comic vein. *La serva padrona* virtually launched the history of the opera buffa. It was, at one and the same time, a perfect realization of its species. Despite the fact that pioneer works are rarely appreciated by their contemporaries, *La serva padrona* was received with tumultuous acclaim.

Pergolesi's life-span was so brief that all his works were created between the years of 1731 and 1736. His health during this period was rapidly disintegrating, so that often composition was made physically impossible because of violent hemorrhages. Yet, despite pain, his production during these five years was prodigious. He worked at a breath-taking pace—as if he realized that he had not long to live. During these few years he composed not only his opera buffa masterpiece, but also eleven other operas, thirty oratorios, psalms, airs, cantatas, four masses, a *Stabat Mater,* four *Salve Reginas,* sonatas, trios, and four volumes of vocal exercises.

In 1734, Pergolesi was engaged by the Duke of Maddaloni as court composer. One year after this, on January 31, 1735, another original work of his was introduced at Rome under his own direction, the opera *L'Olimpiade*. Unfortunately, *L'Olimpiade* was a failure. The audience hissed and stamped its feet in disapproval.

That failure brought on a harrowing period of despondency during which Pergolesi could not find the courage or strength with which to continue the composition of operas. Not until the autumn of 1735 did he produce another opera buffa, *Il flaminio,* presented successfully in Naples.

One of the most poignant incidents in Pergolesi's life took place in or about 1735. It is said—and there are those who believe this is a legend—that he fell in love with Maria Spinelli, a girl of high rank. For a while, he thought of marriage. Maria's brothers, however, swore that if within three days their sister did not vow to renounce the composer forever from her thoughts they would kill him. When, three days later, they returned to their sister for her answer, they discovered that she had surrendered herself to a convent.

To Pergolesi the loss of his loved one was virtually a death-blow. From this time on, his health was doomed.

He suffered so intensely from consumption—his physical pain was as poignant as the mental—that, early in 1736, he was forced to leave for a rest cure in Pozzuoli. It was here (or so it is strongly believed) that he composed his choral masterpiece, the profound and poignant *Stabat Mater,* commissioned by the Confraternity of San Luigi di Palazzo at Naples for the miserable fee of ten ducats. If it is true that the *Stabat Mater* was composed in Pozzuoli, it was created by Pergolesi with the realization that death was near, and it goes a long way towards explaining the source of its many moments of otherworldliness.

For Pergolesi knew he was dying. He knew that the hour for work was drawing to an end. The realization of this made him work with twice his former feverishness. At one time a friend attempted to draw him from his composition, urging him to desist from work even if only for a brief respite. But always Pergolesi replied to such entreaties: "Alas, I can take no rest. I have no time to lose." In this, Pergolesi reminds us strikingly of Mozart who also knew that "the hour is striking," and who also refused to forsake his last compositorial task for the sake of rest.

It is perhaps an eloquent reflection of his temperament that one of Pergolesi's last works, written during hours of excessive pain (his life further darkened by the ever-hovering shadow of imminent death) should have been a vulgar and lusty musical jest: a satire on the Capuchin monks entitled *Scherzo fatto ai Cappuccini di Pozzuoli.*

Giovanni Battista Pergolesi died in Pozzuoli on March 16, 1736, and was buried in the cathedral of that town. The inscription on his grave reads: *Giovane e moribondo* ("young and dying"). A few later biographers attributed his untimely death to poisoning, and some attributed it to a profligate life. But it has since become reasonably certain that neither explanation is based on historic fact, but that he died from consumption.

Pergolesi's most famous works include his cantata *Orfeo,* his eloquent *Stabat Mater,* a few lesser instrumental works, and *La serva padrona.* Without attempting to minimize the significance of his other works (and no one admires his *Stabat Mater* more than this writer), it is *La serva padrona,* unquestionably, which has given Pergolesi his great historic importance.

Some writers have found a close affinity between the musical styles of Pergolesi and Mozart. Such similarity exists, even after one has passed beyond superficial exteriors. Like Mozart's, Pergolesi's style ranged from the sparkling wit of *La serva padrona* to the profundity and pain of the *Stabat Mater,* from an ebullient froth to a beauty that stabs the heart. Like Mozart's, Pergolesi's music was generally characterized by grace, poise, and technical self-assurance. It was always, even in its most humorous moments, elegantly fashioned.

La serva padrona frequently makes the astute listener think of *The Marriage of Figaro.* For like *Figaro,* its fleet dialogue is often punctuated with music that is always crisp, engaging, resilient. This music has Mozartean mobility. The spell of enchantment it creates is never permitted to break. There is an attempt (although more successfully realized by Mozart in *Figaro* than by Pergolesi) at musical characterization; and there is also a successful effort to mould the musical resources of rhythm and tone color to the demands of the text.

The plot of *La serva padrona* is elementary, and revolves about only three characters; there is no chorus, no ballet. Uberto is the master of the house. Serpina is his maid. Vespone (a mute) is the valet. Serpina, weary of being a maid, aspires to become the wife of her master. A carefully contrived plot between herself

[*108*]

and the mute valet finally yields successful results. Uberto falls a victim to the trap and asks for the hand of his maid in marriage.

This is the whole story, told with remarkable simplicity. It unfolds with a lightness of touch which is magically caught by Pergolesi's fleet music. True, *La serva padrona* is a work limited in its scope; but it is of exquisite perfection in every detail of the design. The score sparkles with phosphorescent wit. It was created with such spontaneity that it has never lost the contagious appeal which it exerted on its first audiences. That appeal was still felt strongly when, a few years ago, it was revived in New York City by the Federal Music Project.

With *La serva padrona,* Pergolesi made musical history. Almost single-handed, it created the merry world of the opera buffa, the opéra comique, the comic opera. Twenty years after its first performance in Naples, it was introduced to the rest of Europe by a group of wandering players; everywhere it was received with tumultuous success. We have already seen, in connection with Rameau, what an upheaval was caused in the musical life of Paris by its first performance. So enchanted was Jean Jacques Rousseau by the Pergolesi masterpiece that he was inspired to write a work in a similar vein, *Le Devin du village,* which was first produced in Paris in 1752 with outstanding success. But Rousseau, it might be added, imitated Pergolesi none too successfully. Pergolesi's simplicity he reduced to sheer naïveté, with melodies that often lacked charm or originality.

La serva padrona has exerted as far-reaching an influence on musical development as virtually any single work. Its influence was so profound that an entire generation of composers was tempted by it to essay composition in a similar style. In France, it was directly responsible for the birth of the opéra comique. The first important composer of the opéra comique, Pierre Monsigny, was given direction and viewpoint by Pergolesi's masterpiece. He was born in Frauquemberque, near St. Omer, in France, in 1729, and in his eighteenth year he came to Paris, uncertain of his future. He was passionately fond of music, having studied the violin at the Jesuit College in St. Omer. But he was undecided about making music his career, and while biding his time he worked as a clerk.

Then in 1752—he was twenty-three years of age at the time—he heard Pergolesi's *La serva padrona.* Suddenly his destiny as a musician was revealed to him. He would be a composer of opera buffa! Inspired by Pergolesi, he returned to music study with greater assiduity than ever. He made such progress as a harmony student of Gianotti that in five months' time he was able to submit to his teacher the manuscript of his first work, *Les Aveux indiscrets*. It was a comic opera, and it was performed for the first time at the Théâtre de la Foire on February 7, 1759. Thereafter he composed many works in the lighter style which became the models for future French composers. Monsigny built the comic opera on the outlines established by Pergolesi, but he gave it the flavor of French temperament. Berlioz goes so far as to say that Monsigny was as significant and as genuine in his own field of endeavor as Gluck was in his.

Another prominent composer of the opéra comique was inspired by Pergolesi. He was André Ernest Modeste Grétry, who was born in Liége, Belgium, on February 8, 1741. He was only a boy when he heard *La serva padrona* for the first time. As he later confessed in his memoirs, he "nearly died with pleasure." Like Monsigny, he was inspired by Pergolesi to write lighter music for the theatre. "Pergolesi was the creator," he wrote. "My own music is but a continuation of his."

And after Grétry came the first triumvirate of great composers of the French opéra comique: François Boïeldieu (1775–1834), composer of *La Dame blanche;* Daniel François Auber (1782–1871), whose *Fra Diavolo* is one of the early masterpieces of opéra comique writing; and Adolphe Adam (1803–1856), the creator of *Le Postillon de Longjumeau. . . .*

In Italy, the opera buffa of Pergolesi became a favorite form of the Italian masters, who took to it and exploited it as much as they did the more pretentious opera seria. The Italian opera buffa soon yielded an inexhaustible richness of wit, brightness and merry pace: and it yielded these in such gems as Cimarosa's *Il matrimonio segreto,* Galuppi's *Il filosofo di campagna,* Paisiello's *The Barber of Seville* and Piccinni's *La cecchina.* All these works owe their origin to Pergolesi. From him, their composers learned the use of light and shade in subtle contrasts, the application of rhythm for the enunciation of light, coquettish moods, the chattering bass, and warmth and glow of the harmonization, the fleeting staccato figures, as well as something of the beautifully sculptured perfection of the melodic line. And from these composers we pass directly to that greatest of all masters of the Italian opera buffa, Rossini.

Even in Germany, the influence of Pergolesi was felt. It might well be said that *La serva padrona* inspired the origin of the Singspiel as unmistakably as it helped create the Italian opera buffa and the French opéra comique.

The Singspiel—a comedy interpolated with popular songs and ensemble pieces—is the direct predecessor of the German opera and the ancestor of the German operetta which in later years was to capture the heart and the imagination of the entire world. Its creator was Johann Adam Hiller (1728–1804), distinguished German musician, the founder and first conductor of the famous Leipzig Gewandhaus Orchestra. Gifted in the song-form, and possessing a musical style of considerable charm and deftness, Hiller was indirectly inspired by Pergolesi, and directly by the French opéra comique, to bring his gifts into the theatre. His wonderful flair for wit and his ingratiating appeal made his theatrical works, or Singspiel as he called them, favorites of the masses. His popular melodies were sung, as Burney remarked, "by all classes of people, and some of them in the streets." Of course, even the best of his Singspiel had artistic limitations. Such works as *Lottchen auf Hofe, Die Jagd,* or *Der Teufel ist los* were little more than humorous skits with music. But these works were fertile soil on which later German composers cultivated their greatest works. The Hiller Singspiel, after subtle transformations at the hands of Reichardt, and other lesser German composers, was soon to be transformed into a form of limitless proportions by Mozart.

Thus comic opera everywhere was either directly, or by subtle indirect influence, to be given shape and direction by Pergolesi's *La serva padrona*. *La serva padrona* virtually began the history of the comic opera. Rarely has any movement begun so significantly with a pioneer achievement.

II

EARLY INSTRUMENTAL MUSIC

Arcangelo Corelli

Domenico Scarlatti

Johann Kuhnau

François Couperin

Johann Joseph Fux

Antonio Caldara

THE *Nuove musiche* which the Florentine "camerata" evolved, set into motion the new era of music known as the homophonic period. This period stands apart from the age which preceded it—namely, the polyphonic era—by giving prominence not to several voices of equal importance but to a single significant voice. From such a revolutionary departure arose the opera. More important still, there now arose modern instrumental music.

In the beginning there was the organ.

One of the first great masters of organ music—perhaps the most significant of the pioneers who preceded Johann Sebastian Bach—was Dietrich Buxtehude. There were important composers of organ music before Buxtehude: Frescobaldi, for example, was the first composer for the organ to realize successfully an *instrumental* style of music writing as opposed to the vocal. But not even Frescobaldi brought to organ forms such magnificent realization, such a consummation of their powers, as Buxtehude did.

The silence with which the world of music permitted the tercentenary of Buxtehude to pass in 1937 emphasized at the time the lamentable neglect suffered by one of the great creative masters, and one of the most potent historic forces, that the history of music has known. During the tercentenary year a few scattered articles were published in magazines attempting to call attention to the greatness of a forgotten master; and a new biography—in German—appeared. But these were feeble gestures in attempting to restore the music of a master to the concert hall where it so well belonged and from which it has for so long a time been so noticeably absent. Only one major Buxtehude composition received wide performance in America that year—a *Passacaglia,* featured by the Philadelphia Orchestra in an orchestral arrangement by Lucien Cailliet. Only two Buxtehude compositions were pressed on phonograph discs—and these by a small and independent company. When this information is coupled with the fact that, in recent years, a performance of a work by Buxtehude has been so rare as to strain the memory; also that altogether only half a dozen or so morsels have ever been reproduced on phonograph records (with many lesser composers so generously represented) —when all this is taken into consideration, it becomes apparent how appalling has been the obscurity of a composer who should be recognized as one of music's major figures.

He should be recognized as a major figure in music because he created many works extraordinary in their imagination. He should also be recognized as one of music's most gallant pioneers, one who was ready to try new forms and styles which were only sparsely in use in his time, and to enrich these so incalculably that he remains the only major predecessor of Johann Sebastian Bach.

Johann Sebastian Bach inherited the oratorio of Carissimi after it had passed through the hands, and acquired the identifying fingerprints, of many other composers. But many of these organ forms in which Bach produced his greatest works were acquired by him directly from Buxtehude. Alfred Einstein, who is not given to excessive statements, has written that Bach's passacaglia "would not have existed without Buxtehude." Even though one wishes to speak cautiously, one can hardly resist the suspicion that to Buxtehude Bach owed his use of other organ forms as well —principally, the chorale-prelude, the toccata and the

chaconne. None of these forms was invented by Buxtehude himself. And yet, as forms into which a composer
can pour the torrent of his creative genius, they really
first came into their own with Buxtehude.

The passacaglia and the chaconne were both old
dances. Many organists of the eighteenth century used
these forms as a means with which to display their virtuosity as performers, as well as to exhibit their compositorial skill in fashioning ingenious variations to a
given theme for ground bass. But Buxtehude knew
that these forms were capable of artistic expressiveness
far beyond anything achieved by his contemporaries or
predecessors; and with Buxtehude these forms became
the settings for artistic messages of profound implica-
tions.

The chorale-prelude was also in use before Buxtehude. Certainly, Buxtehude added nothing techni-
cally to a form first used effectively by Sweelinck (1562–
1621), then brought to high development by Samuel
Scheidt (1587–1654). And yet, with both Sweelinck
and Scheidt, the chorale-prelude was little more than a
free fantasia on a given melody, once again helping to
display the virtuosity of the organ performer. But with
Buxtehude it became, without changing its form, a
medium for poetic musing, an eloquent musical poem

with a beautifully sustained mood—a subjective expression of a deeply religious soul.

And the toccata found its first master in Frescobaldi, who proved how brilliant a show-piece it could become in exploiting the fleet fingers of the virtuoso. But Buxtehude, more than Frescobaldi, revealed to Bach that the toccata was much more than a display piece; he revealed to Bach, in his own toccatas, that it was capable of far-reaching musical drama together with its brilliant technical effects, that it could be made into an architectonic design of large proportions, with an almost cathedral-like majesty.

How significant Buxtehude's music was in the formation of Bach's own works may best be understood by comparing the greatest of Buxtehude's works with those of his predecessors. Only then do we notice how Buxtehude alone, of all these composers, most nearly approached the Leipzig master in the consummate skill of form and the endless wealth of inventive genius. While one is ready to accept much in the music of Frescobaldi, Froberger, Pachelbel, Samuel Scheidt, and the others, which has fascination—a comparison of these composers with Buxtehude reveals in these earlier musicians an inventive faculty of a lesser order. To compare a toccata or a fugue by Frescobaldi or Fro-

berger with one by Buxtehude is very much like plac-
ing a basilica at the side of St. Peter's. Both Frescobaldi
and Froberger had a consummate feeling for form, and
their writing is often adroit. But only Bach was Buxtehude's superior in translating the constraining form of
the fugue and the superficial glitter of the toccata into
human experience, in infusing into their formerly lifeless skeletons the pulse and heart-beat, the flesh and
muscle of a human organism. The E-minor chaconne
of Buxtehude, for example, may not be of the Gargantuan stature of the famous solo violin chaconne of
Bach; yet in its eloquent opening measures it is no
minor poet who is speaking but a creator of epic
stature.

Buxtehude was at his greatest in those forms which
were, more or less, embryonic when he found them,
and which he developed into formidable proportions
before passing them on to their ultimate master, Bach.
The forms included the chorale-prelude, the passacaglia, the chaconne, and the toccata. In these forms,
where imaginative treatment is of greater importance
than technical skill, Buxtehude towered over his predecessors. His inventiveness in the manipulation of melodic material, his phenomenal capacity to suggest
subtle contrasts of color, mood and emotion, to build

climactic effects in the variation-form of his chaconnes and passacaglias—all this would have been considered extraordinary even if Buxtehude had followed Bach instead of preceding him. As it is, with Buxtehude's greatest works composed before Bach attained maturity, Buxtehude must rank as one of the major masters in musical history.

Buxtehude's whole manipulation of detail, harmony, phraseology and structure is singularly mature and full of life [wrote C. Hubert Parry in the *Oxford History of Music*]. The breadth and scope of his works, his power of putting things in their right places, his daring invention, the brilliancy of his figuration, the beauty and strength of his harmony, and above all a strange tinge of romanticism which permeated his disposition, as Spitta has justly observed, marked him as one of the greatest composers of organ music, except the one and only Johann Sebastian Bach. And in Johann Sebastian Bach's organ works the traces of the influence of Buxtehude are more plentiful than those of any other composer. It is not too much to say that unless Dietrich Buxtehude had gone before, the world would have had to do without some of the most lovable and interesting traits in the divinest and the most exquisitely human of all composers.

The form in which Buxtehude is generally conceded to have achieved his most felicitous expression is the chorale-prelude which he inherited from Scheidt and Pachelbel, and which became in his hands an eloquent fragment drenched with religious feeling, ennobled by a high and moving spirit of poetry. And what a wealth of imagination Buxtehude brought to the decoration of his melodies, which was of the most delicate embroidery! Cecil Gray realized the importance of the Buxtehude chorale-prelude when he wrote:

> The chorale prelude was raised to an unexemplified pitch of elaboration, and enriched with every conceivable device of contrapuntal and decorative resource at his disposal. In his hands, indeed, the theme is frequently so varied and adorned with arabesques as to become totally unrecognizable and even when presented textually, it is often hidden from sight altogether under the exuberant welter of ornamentation with which it is surrounded.

Musicologists have long accepted the far-reaching influence of Buxtehude on Bach. We have already quoted Parry and Einstein's statements in which they pointed to Bach's debt to his forerunner. Other writers have also strummed a similar theme. "As John the Baptist was to Christ," wrote A. Eaglefield Hull, "so was . . . Buxtehude to Bach." Charles Sanford Terry emphasized the fact that in Buxtehude Bach "found a powerful stimulus and a great example."

Yet to the fastidious music lover, the name of Buxtehude remains only faintly familiar; and his music—so often inexhaustible in ideas and in the variety of the style—is virtually unknown.

But a word, first, about those early masters of organ music who preceded Buxtehude and sharpened for him the necessary tools of organ composition.

The first important composers of organ music—contrapuntists like Andrea and Giovanni Gabrieli (uncle and nephew) and Jan Sweelinck, all of whom lived from the close of the sixteenth century through the beginning of the seventeenth—wrote for the organ as if they were writing for human voices. That an instrument required an altogether different style of music—

less attentive to the fluidity of the melodic line, and more to variety of color and nuance, and to rhythmic flexibility—was not recognized until Girolamo Frescobaldi. Frescobaldi may, therefore, well be said to have been the father of the instrumental style for the organ. As such, he set the stage for Buxtehude.

Frescobaldi was born in Ferrara, Italy, in September of 1583. He was a child prodigy, and was exhibited in organ recitals (as well as in vocal performances) throughout Italy. He studied under Luzzaschi, one of the most distinguished organists of the time. Then, in early manhood, Frescobaldi visited the Netherlands where he came into contact with its contrapuntal school, and where he published his first important work—a book of five-part madrigals.

When he returned to Italy, Frescobaldi became the organist of St. Peter's in Rome. He was only twenty-five years old at the time. Yet his fame as a performer on the organ was already so great that music lovers came from far and wide (some thirty thousand of them) to hear his first performance at St. Peter's. In 1628, Frescobaldi took an extended leave-of-absence from Rome to visit Florence, where for five years he was private organist to the Grand Duke of Tuscany. A plague in Florence then brought him back to his post at St. Peter's, where he now remained until the end of his life.

As the years passed, his stature as organist grew until there was no one in all of Europe who could equal his fame or match his powers. His contemporaries spoke of him as "the marvel of the age"; they said of him that he could play the organ better with hands crossed than anyone else in a natural position. And the venerable historian, Ambros, looks upon Frescobaldi as the first in that great classic period of organ playing which produced such masters as Buxtehude and Johann Sebastian Bach.

Frescobaldi died in Rome on March 1, 1643; he died passing on his influence and his traditions to a deserving pupil, Johann Froberger.

Frescobaldi composed many works for the organ: toccatas, fugues, caprices, partitas, and so on. The twentieth century ear finds in these works great technical astuteness, but only rarely that strength of beauty, that power of invention which bring to Buxtehude his deathless modernity. And yet one should be careful not to underestimate Frescobaldi. When we hear him at his greatest—one must acknowledge that his famous *Toccata for the Elevation* is a masterpiece, a work magnificent in its breadth of style—we are tempted to wonder if Buxtehude would have been possible without Frescobaldi. For Frescobaldi was one of the first composers of organ music to touch his works with human feelings; he was one of the first organ composers to achieve a style beautifully suited for his instrument, a style "free from vocal tyranny"; he was one of the first to give clarity to such organ forms as the toccata and the fugue.

From Frescobaldi, organ music passed on to Johann Froberger; and from Froberger the line that stretched to Buxtehude crosses Samuel Scheidt, who evolved modern organ notation, and Johann Schein (1586–1630), who successfully transplanted the Italian instrumental style into Germany.

The biographical material available on Buxtehude is not copious, and often its ancestry is questionable. It is believed that he was born in 1637, and the place of his birth was Helsinborg, Sweden (not Helsingör, as was so long believed by historians). Buxtehude came of German stock that had migrated from the small village of Buxtehude, between Bremen and Hamburg. His father was, before 1641, organist at the Marienkirche in Helsinborg, and after that the organist at the Olaikirche in Helsingör (Shakespeare's *Elsinore*), to which city the Buxtehude family had transferred its home when Dietrich was still a child.

From his father, Dietrich received most of his musical education. When this was completed, Buxtehude became organist at the Marienkirche in the city of his birth (holding this post between the years of 1657 and 1660). His salary was a meager one—seventy-five thaler a year with an additional thaler for the coal used in the organ loft. It was in this post that Buxtehude first attracted attention to his great virtuosity as organist.

In 1660, Buxtehude became the organist of the Marienkirche in Helsingör at a salary more than double that which he had previously received. But Helsingör, as well as Helsinborg, was merely the preparation ground for an assignment in which Buxtehude was to achieve his full stature both as organist and as composer.

On April 11, 1668, Buxtehude was elected organist and *Werkmeister* of the St. Mary Church at Lübeck, succeeding Franz Tunder, whose daughter Buxtehude married in conformance with the prescribed rules. As *Werkmeister*, Buxtehude was something of a Pooh-Bah of the church. He was Official Receiver, who kept the records of baptisms, marriages, births, deaths, and burials. He was Treasurer, who kept accounts of all money due to the church and expended by it. He was the Inspector of the Building, and had to report on all necessary repairs. He had to look after the church wine, the church linen, the church cleaning. And this was but a fraction of his duties. For these menial functions—and for the job of playing the organ, which was considered only one of many duties—Buxtehude was paid the generous sum of one thousand marks a year. And there were compensations other than monetary at Lübeck: the organ, with its three manuals and fifty-four stops, was one of the best in Germany, even though it was in need of overhauling.

It was in this position that Buxtehude (at the same time that he attended to a thousand and one details of church administration) achieved his great reputation, principally as an organ performer, and secondly as a composer for that instrument. For forty years, Buxtehude's organ playing attracted pilgrims from many parts of Europe. It is well known that Johann Sebastian Bach made the journey from Arnstadt to Lübeck in 1705 (whether he made the journey on foot, as some historians have said, is a questionable point). Bach was so dazzled by Buxtehude's genius that he prolonged his leave-of-absence from Arnstadt to become Buxtehude's pupil. Charles Sanford Terry has confirmed the

far-reaching influence of Buxtehude on the young
Bach:

> The Lübeck visit is of high importance in
> the development of Bach's genius. It confirmed
> impressions formed at Lüneburg, and gave him
> a conception of music's relation to public wor-
> ship which never left him, an ideal tardily real-
> ized at Leipzig. . . . Not infrequently, we may
> be sure, he played . . . at the console behind
> the organ façade splendidly poised above the
> western arch of the Marienkirche, receiving the
> commendation and advice of one whose genius
> was touched by the poetic fire that lit his own.
> In this stimulating intercourse the weeks sped
> unheeded.

And Bach was not the only one to come paying homage to a master. Shortly after Bach's visit, Handel, in
the company of Mattheson, made a pilgrimage to Lübeck.

During his forty years at Lübeck, Buxtehude played
the organ and performed his own works in which the
forms of the toccata, passacaglia and chaconne, and the
chorale-prelude acquired new life and character. When
Johann Sebastian Bach was appointed organist at the

Ducal Chapel at Weimar (during which period he composed his greatest works for organ), Buxtehude had been dead a year; but his music was still vibrantly alive, exerting a subtle and inescapable spell over the younger composer.

During these forty years, too, Buxtehude conducted a series of concerts which he called *Abendmusiken,* given on five Sundays prior to Christmas. These concerts, for which a small admission was charged, may be said to have been one of the earliest types of public concert performances. These *Abendmusiken* became famous throughout Europe, and it is for these affairs that Buxtehude composed the greatest amount of his vocal and instrumental music which, in their own way, are as remarkable examples of Buxtehude's creative powers as his organ music.

Dietrich Buxtehude died in Lübeck on May 9, 1707. It is said that both Bach and Handel were considered his possible successors at Lübeck. It is also said that both of them refused to abide by the rules which specified that the successor must marry Buxtehude's daughter. Whether this is so, has never been authoritatively substantiated. In any case, though Bach did not succeed Buxtehude at the organ at Lübeck, he became his successor as a composer for that instrument.

§ 2

THE earliest solo instrumental music was for the organ. But it was well before Buxtehude's death that music was written for other instruments as well. One of the earliest, and possibly the first successful, composers of the instrumental sonata was Arcangelo Corelli.

It is generally believed that the title of "sonata" was first used by Bonifazio Graziani in the sixteenth century. It was used by the early Italian composers as a term denoting the instrumental counterpart of the cantata. The cantata was a composition to be *sung,* and, therefore, featured the voice and accompanying instruments; the sonata, on the other hand, was a composition to be *sounded,* or *played,* and was built around a solo instrument, or a group of instruments, and an accompaniment.

The sonata was developed from the canzona, an early instrumental form written in the polyphonic style known as "strict imitation." As early as 1600, Giovanni Gabrieli composed canzone for quartet and double quartet which imitated the *a cappella* singing in the church for musical instruments. Soon the terms canzona and sonata became interchangeable; and before very long the name of sonata completely displaced that of canzona for instrumental music.

The immediate successor of the canzona was the sonata da chiesa—or an instrumental sonata suitable for the church. In form it usually consisted of a broad and majestic introduction followed by a *fugato* passage; then came a short *largo* which also culminated in a light *fugato*. The earlier works in this form combined these four sections into one integrated composition, while with later composers these sections became separate and independent movements. Thus the sonata da chiesa is the accepted forerunner of the later sonata. It was generally written for a group of instruments accompanied by an organ. There was also a secular sonata, or sonata da camera, which consisted of a grouping of dances. This was later to develop into the suite.

A yawning gap stretches between the sonatas of Corelli and the accepted sonata form of Haydn and Mozart. Yet the latter would hardly have been made possible without the existence of the former. In his sonatas, which he wrote in both the "camera" and the "chiesa" forms, Corelli, more than any of his predecessors, created an instrumental style which, though still polyphonic in character, succeeded in bringing the same importance to the individual instrument that the opera had brought to the individual singer.

The first four published works of Corelli, appearing between 1680 and 1694—sonatas for two instruments and a figured bass—become one of the solid foundations upon which later chamber music writing is to rest. The epoch-making Opus 5—his sonatas for violin and accompaniment—becomes the source of all future sonata writing for violin and piano. And in the Opus 6 still another new world is explored by him: that of the concerto grosso, one of the most important forerunners of the concerto form.

His name was Arcangelo, or "arch-angel"; but his contemporaries called him the "arch-devil" because of his diabolic skill in playing the violin. Those who heard him felt that when he put violin to chin and bow to strings he was having communion with the lower world. They remarked that, as he played, a physical transformation took place with him: his countenance, they said, became "distorted," his eyes became "red as fire," and his eyeballs "rolled in agony." Of course they spoke rapturously of his aristocratic style as an interpreter, his beautiful singing tone, his flexible technique, and the fire and brilliance of his personality. But most of all they spoke of his incredible, his superhuman powers over his instrument. They said of him—just as later audiences were to say of Paganini—that technique such as his could have its origin only with the devil himself.

He was, truth to tell, the first of that long and magisterial line of interpreters on the violin which was to extend through Paganini and Joachim to Heifetz and Kreisler. As J. B. Cartier has written:

> Before Corelli, the art of playing the violin was completely ignored. The performance on that instrument was relegated to the routine of musicians who could hardly qualify under the title of honorable artists.

And Paul Stoeving has written more recently:

> It is Corelli who has raised the art of fiddling to the dignity of an art.

It is important to speak of his greatness as virtuoso. For when he turned to composing music for his instrument, he wrote as one who knew fully and intimately the resources of the violin. Not that he wrote works in the vein of Paganini, exacting in their difficulties. As a matter of fact, Corelli never wrote beyond the third position, and never asked for gymnastics on the part of the performer. But better than anyone before him he knew how to write music that lay gracefully on the fingerboard of the instrument, music which was meant for the violin alone and which, for the first time, made of the violin a reputable virtuoso instrument.

Arcangelo Corelli was born in Fusignano, near Imola, on February 12, 1653. He was first taught music by Matteo Simonelli, a singer in the pontifical choir. Because church music held almost no appeal for the young student, he soon changed his teacher, and went for instruction to that Italian master of graceful song, Bassani. Bassani gave Corelli an intensive training on the violin. Corelli took to the violin with natural aptitude, acquiring such mastery that by 1672—he was only nineteen at the time—his fame spread far and wide throughout Europe. It was even said by John Hawkins (though one questions the accuracy of his statement) that Corelli was compelled to return to Italy from Paris, on his concert tour, through the cabals and intrigues of Lully who was afraid that Corelli's great fame might eclipse his own in France.

In 1680, Corelli toured Germany and was magnificently received by the German princes. For two years he remained in the service of the Elector of Bavaria. When he returned to Rome, he published his first work, a collection of twelve sonatas for two violins and an accompanying bass.

In or about 1700, Corelli became the leader of an opera orchestra in Rome. His fame was now at its peak. (No less a musician than Alessandro Scarlatti rhapsodically sang his praises!) He was the favored son of the highest society in Rome. Cardinal Pietro Ottoboni was his patron and most intimate friend. Cardinal Ottoboni, nephew of a Pope, was one of the most famous patrons of the age. At his palace gathered the intellectual élite of Rome who, together with the Cardinal, spent tireless hours in talking about art. The Cardinal spent money lavishly—and most lavishly of all on music. For he adored music, and he spread gifts bountifully on the beggar-musician in the street and the neglected genius in his garret.

He virtually adopted Corelli, poured on him munificent gifts and luxuries in return for the great music Corelli brought him. At the palace of the Cardinal, Corelli made his home until the end of his life, conducting important concerts there every Monday evening.

Strange to say, this musician, who enjoyed a fame second to none during the greater part of his life, was soon to experience years of melancholy. He saw younger violinists, whose technique now was more facile than his, usurping the limelight; and he, who had known the limelight for so many years, could not accept this eclipse gracefully. One evening he attended a concert in which an oboist was given a tumultuous ovation. This so embittered him that he swore never again to appear in public. Even his former great success as a composer was being obscured by the rising light of such a young composer as Valentini. Envy embittered the closing years of his life. He grew sullen and depressed.

He died, a broken and unhappy man, on January 10, 1713, and was buried in the Pantheon in Rome. For many years after his death, the anniversary of his death was commemorated by musical performances at his grave.

The Corelli instrumental sonatas which comprise his first four published volumes form the basis of all future chamber music writing. Though there existed scattered examples of chamber music before Corelli published his Opus 1 (there are those who trace the earliest string-quartet to Gregorio. Allegri in the early part of the seventeenth century), none before Corelli so completely realized chamber music style.

It is not necessary here to analyze the structure of Corelli's trios, for it is not in their structure that these works are important. Only one element of Corelli's form should interest us. In several movements of his trios he supplements a first subject with a second one of a contrasting nature, thereby giving suggestion of the contrasting second theme of the later school.

However, in his instrumental style—and a style which he achieved at a time when instrumental music was yet in its infancy!—his importance is historic. His melodic ideas are inexhaustible in their variety. His modulations are sensitive and natural. With an admirable sense for form, everything "sits right" in his music. Above all, his writing—polyphonic in character, for the most part—has remarkable lucidity.

With his lucidity, Corelli more than any composer before his time, taught musicians how to write most effectively for a small combination of instruments. With it he achieved that purity and transparency of writing which might well be said to be the goal towards which chamber music must always reach.

His Opus 5 is equally epoch-making, for it is the pioneer work from which stem all future sonatas for the violin and piano. Even when he wrote for solo instrument and accompanying bass, Corelli's style was polyphonic. And though the violin does not lend itself naturally to polyphonic writing, Corelli emancipated the violin as a solo instrument. To analyze the twelve sonatas of Opus 5 is to realize how wonderfully Corelli exploited the capacities of the violin to speak its own musical language. The bow arm acquired, probably for the first time, the flexibility and resilience of which it is capable—as, for example, in the justly famous *La Folia* variations. His music is equally well written for the left hand, understanding its weakness and strength.

But if one thing stands out vividly in the Corelli sonatas for two instruments it is the quality of his slow movements, in which he brought to the violin its inborn capacity to sing. His adagios—the adagio of the Sixth Sonata is a particularly apt example—are frequently touched with a beauty of indescribable warmth and intensity of feeling. These slow movements are sometimes introspective, sometimes sharp with pain,

[*141*]

most often full-throated with lyricism like the best arias of Alessandro Scarlatti. From Corelli, all later composers for the violin learned the art of writing slow movements which soar on the wings of song.

His Opus 7 is one of the great pioneer experiments in the writing of the concerto grosso. Concerto was a term first employed by Ludovico Viadana in 1602 when he called a series of motets for voice and organ *concerti ecclesiastici*. But the concerto was soon adopted by the Italian composers not for voices but for groupings of instruments. In 1686, Giuseppe Torelli published a concerto da camera for two violins and a figured bass; this, however, was hardly more than another designation for the then-existing sonata da camera.

Corelli, on the other hand, developed a distinct concerto grosso style, a model for such succeeding composers as Geminiani, Vivaldi, and even Handel. He established the instrumentation of the concerto grosso so permanently that even Handel was not to vary from it. His use of light and shade to give contrasting color to his principal themes became one of the essential traits of all concerti grossi. But most important was the clear and unmistakable definition he gave to the concerto grosso form as a whole. The concerto grosso became, in his hands, a pretentious work in which an independent group of solo instruments was contrasted with the *tutti* of the entire orchestra, one set off against the other, and then combined in impressive and powerful climaxes.

From the use of a *group* of solo instruments against the background of an orchestra to that of a *single* solo instrument is but a step which Italian composers were not slow to take. Thus out of Corelli's concerto grosso grew the concerto for solo instrument and orchestra of Tartini, Valentini, Vivaldi, Handel, and Johann Sebastian Bach.

It is impossible to exaggerate Corelli's importance in the history of music. From him came modern chamber music. In England, Henry Purcell—among the first masters of instrumental writing—was inspired to write his first set of trios on a model of Corelli (published in 1683)—as Henry Playford pointed out in his famous couplet:

> *In thy productions we with wonder find*
> *Bassani's genius to Corelli join'd.*

In France, the father of French instrumental music, François Couperin-le-Grand openly confessed his indebtedness to Corelli and acknowledged the parentage

of his first French instrumental sonatas, composed in
1692, to the Italian master:

> The first sonata in this collection was also the
> first which I composed, and which anyone has
> composed in France. Its history is singular.
> Charmed by those works by Corelli, whose com-
> positions I have loved as long as I lived . . . I
> attempted to compose one, which I had per-
> formed at that very concert where I first heard
> those of Corelli.

The German, Georg Telemann (1681–1767) openly
confessed in his autobiography that he freely used
Corelli as the model for his own chamber music; and
Telemann was the composer of many interesting sonatas, trios, and even quartets. After Telemann, chamber music required only a more intimate association
with the then-evolving sonata form (and it received
such association at the hands of Johann Stamitz and
Johann Christian Bach) to be prepared for its fullest
exploitation by the first masters of the string quartet—
Dittersdorf, Boccherini, and Joseph Haydn. . . .

From Corelli, too, there grew modern violin music
—the violin sonata and the violin concerto. In Italy,
Corelli created an entire school of composers, which in-

cluded such masters as Tartini, Veracini, Geminiani, and Vivaldi, all of whom learned from him how to write for the violin and who, through their own works, produced a great literature which forms the basis of all violin music. Once these composers had given a new importance to music for the violin, such masters as Handel and Bach could enrich the repertoire further with their own sonatas and concertos.

IT WAS not long after Corelli published his Opus 1 that there arose a composer to write the first sonata for solo piano (or, to speak more accurately, the clavier, parent of the piano).

When discussion arises concerning the early history of the piano sonata, the well-informed musician will inevitably mention names such as Domenico Scarlatti or the more famous of Bach's sons—Wilhelm Friedemann, Karl Philipp Emanuel, and Johann Christian. These composers, and others as well, produced outstanding examples of early piano sonatas, some of which are still occasionally performed in the concert hall.

Yet the inventor of the piano sonata is not among the above-mentioned composers. He is, rather, a half-forgotten German master, one of the foremost musicians of his day, the first to apply successfully the use of the sonata to the piano of his time.

His name is Johann Kuhnau. In musical history his

name is prominent by virtue of the fact that he was the immediate predecessor of Johann Sebastian Bach at the Thomasschule in Leipzig. But a greater distinction than this is his. Had Kuhnau never lived, or had he never experimented in the writing of sonatas for the keyboard instrument, we might today have been deprived of that remarkable literature which includes all the great sonatas from Scarlatti to those of our own day.

His celebrated contemporary, Johann Mattheson, wrote the following glowing appraisal of Kuhnau:

> The name of Kuhnau can be inscribed on three levels of our musical monument. He was a fine organist, a learned scholar and a great musician, composer and chorus-director.

But Mattheson did not go far enough in his evaluation of the German master. Kuhnau was one of the first to recognize what an important role the keyboard instrument could perform in music, the first to suggest that a great library of music could be written for that unexplored instrument, the first to evolve a new technique for writing for such an instrument. Couperin (often called the father of keyboard music by virtue of his extraordinary pieces for the harpsichord) published his first *Pièces de clavecin* in 1716. Yet, as early as 1695, Kuhnau published his *Frische Klavier Früchte*. But it is equally important to notice that Kuhnau was the first composer to write a sonata for the piano. Domenico Scarlatti did not compose his own sonatas for piano until more than two decades after Kuhnau first published his.

Johann Kuhnau was born in Bohemia, in the town of Geising, in April of 1660—twenty-five years before the birth of Bach, Handel, and Domenico Scarlatti. Though Bohemian by birth, Kuhnau is German as a result of an almost lifelong existence in that country. When he was nine years old, he was sent to Dresden to enter the Kreuzschule. There he was a pupil of Jacob Bental and Alexander Hering. He was a brilliant student. It was not long before the Kapellmeister, Vincenzo Albrici, took a personal interest in him and adopted him.

Kuhnau's musical education continued for the next eleven years in Dresden. When an epidemic broke out in that city—in the year of 1680—he went to Zittau where he not only continued his study of music but also entered the University for the study of law. In Zittau, Kuhnau's musical talent first attracted attention. During a municipal election, he was invited to compose a special musical composition. His motet for two choirs received such a spontaneous ovation that Kuhnau was then and there offered the post of cantor. This he accepted, and filled reputably.

Zittau was, after all, only a provincial town, and it soon cramped the ambitious Kuhnau in search of new and greater worlds of activity. After two years, therefore, he left for Leipzig to complete there his law studies at the University. In 1688, he became a lawyer. The practice of law, however, did not altogether remove him from music. He served as organist of the Thomasschule, and in the same year that he entered the legal profession he became more actively engaged in the musical life of the city by founding the Collegium Musicum which sponsored a series of public concerts.

During the next thirteen years, Kuhnau pursued both the practice of law and music—and with equal industry. But he did not confine his gifts to these two activities alone. He was probably the most versatile man in the history of music. He had a knife-edged intellect and a profundity of scholarship rare among the composers of his or any other age. He was a brilliant linguist, a scholar in both Hebrew and Greek. He was a student in mathematics, and he dabbled in science. He translated several books from the Italian and French. And, in the free moments he could snatch from these varied pursuits, he wrote a satiric romance which inspired the praises of a critic no less discriminating than Romain Rolland.

We now come to the year 1695 when Kuhnau published a set of piano pieces entitled *Frische Klavier Früchte.* In itself this event would have been significant because virtuoso pieces for a keyboard instrument other than the organ were, at the time, few and far between; the clavier was not seriously considered at the time an instrument worthy of solo music. But even greater importance is attached to Kuhnau's publication because it contains, for the first time, a sonata for the piano. As Kuhnau himself inquired in the preface to these piano pieces: "Why should not one try to write for the piano in a form which has been utilized for other instruments?"

It is of interest to quote that preface in greater detail, for in it Kuhnau explains his purpose in writing a sonata, and clarifies his mission.

I have employed the same liberty as that employed by Nature when, hanging the fruit on the trees, she gives one branch less or more than others. . . . It did not take me long to produce these pieces: It was with me just as it is in certain countries where, thanks to the unusual heat, everything grows with such rapidity that the harvest may be reaped a month after sowing. While writing the seven sonatas, I experienced such eagerness that without neglecting my other occupations, I wrote on every day, so that this work, which I began on Monday, was completed by the Monday of the following week. I mention these circumstances merely so that no one shall expect to find in them rare exceptional qualities. It is true that we are not always craving for extraordinary things; we often eat the simplest fruits of our fields with as much pleasure as the rarest and most exquisite foreign fruits, although the latter may be very costly or come from a great distance. . . . My fruits are at the disposal of all; those who do not find them to their taste have only to seek elsewhere. As for critics, they will not spare them; but the venom of the ignorant is powerless to injure them any more than a cool dew will harm the ripened fruit.

Seven of Kuhnau's sonatas appeared in the *Frische Klavier Früchte;* six others were grouped under the heading of a later publication entitled *Musical Representations of Some Stories of the Bible,* which contains the famous *Combat Between David and Goliath* still performed by the more adventurous of present-day pianists. *The Combat,* following as it does a detailed program, is frequently accepted by the historian as one of the first successful examples of early programmatic music.

Kuhnau's sonatas for the clavier were usually in three, four, or five movements. While the resemblance between a Kuhnau sonata and one by Joseph Haydn is remote, it is not altogether impossible to trace the seed which was ultimately to produce the full flower. Kuhnau, in his sonatas, frequently demonstrated the use of contrasting moods, often using a slow movement between two fast ones. Occasionally, too, Kuhnau used two themes of a contrasting nature in one movement. Finally, in his sense for form, in the grace with which he developed his musical material, and in the fluidity of his self-expression, he definitely developed the resources of early writing for the piano, and set a pattern which his contemporaries and immediate succes-

sors were not slow in accepting. As Romain Rolland
pointed out:

> He did indeed possess a depth of form, a grace
> compounded of strength and lucidity which
> even today would make his name a household
> word—if society were capable of taking a genu-
> ine interest in music without being urged to do
> so by fashion.

It was inevitable for the sons of Bach (who brought
the piano sonata to further development) to come into
contact with the works of Kuhnau, which they learned
by rote in their music study. For Kuhnau was considered a master in his own day, one of the most respected composers of his generation. Johann Adolf
Scheibe, the eminent musicologist of the eighteenth
century, regarded him as one of the four greatest composers of the time. And Johann Sebastian Bach himself
was known to esteem Kuhnau with no little reverence
and passed this reverence on to his sons.

On May 6, 1701, Johann Kuhnau was offered the
foremost musical post of the city—but on the express
condition that he renounce the practice of law permanently. The post of cantor of the world-famous Tho-

masschule was too attractive to be declined. In 1701, Kuhnau bade farewell to his legal work and devoted himself now to music. For the next twenty years he directed the famous choir of the Thomasschule, arranged public concerts in Leipzig, and devoted himself to composition during which he produced innumerable chorales, cantatas, and passions. It has been pointed out by some Bach students that this choral music of Kuhnau made its influence felt noticeably on the creative growth of Bach.

The closing years of Johann Kuhnau's life were embittered by tragedy. Two sons and a daughter came to a premature death. Kuhnau died in Leipzig on June 25, 1722. He was succeeded in his post at the Thomasschule by Johann Sebastian Bach.

Famous critics have sung the praises of Johann Kuhnau. Philipp Spitta and Shedlock have traced the enormous influence of Kuhnau on the art of both Bach and Handel. Camille Bellaigue has written that program music, while it existed before Kuhnau's time, was never so felicitously expressed. But, in the last analysis, he is best remembered for his achievements as a composer for the piano. By being one of the earliest pioneers to discover the new world of piano music, and by being the first composer to create a sonata for the piano, he set a cornerstone for what has since become one of the most formidable columns in the temple of music.

Although François Couperin-le-Grand did not compose any sonatas for the piano, piano writing achieved at his hands such articulateness that he cannot be excluded when the development of the piano sonata is traced. Wanda Landowska speaks of Couperin as the Chopin of the harpsichord, because, like Chopin,

> Couperin created a style and a technique of his own. Also, like Chopin, he is great not only for what he brings to his instrument in the way of creative gifts, but also for what he draws from it. The capacities of the instrument are wonderfully extended and immeasurably increased by this early French master who must always be considered by the historian as one of the earliest great composers for the piano.[1]

François Couperin-le-Grand (so-called to distinguish him from the elder Couperin, his uncle) came from a magnificent dynasty of musicians which for two centuries had been prominent in the musical life of France. He

[1] In an interview with the author.

was born in Paris on November 10, 1668, and his place of birth was one of the annexes of the St. Gervais Church, the church of which his father was organist. Couperin first studied the organ with his father, and then with Jacques Denis Thomelin of the King's Chapel.

In his twenty-fifth year he entered the King's service. Soon after this a competition was held to decide the new organist for the Chapel Royal. Couperin entered the contest, and was selected by a body of judges which included Louis XIV himself. It was not long before Couperin's outstanding qualities both at the organ and at the harpsichord made him the favorite musician at court. He was appointed *joueur de clavecin de la musique de la chambre du roi* and he served as personal music teacher for those princes closest to the throne. He even became the personal music master to Louis XIV, directing concerts for him at Versailles. For these concerts, Couperin composed his *Concerts royaux* which, during the last years of the King's life, were given regular performances every Sunday with Couperin himself officiating at the harpsichord.

When Louis XIV died, Couperin's association with Versailles became less intimate. He went into comparative retirement, substituting intimate recitals at his home in place of his former royal concerts at the palace. At his home in the Palais Royal section of Paris he died on September 12, 1733.

Couperin's *Concerts royaux* represent the earliest successful attempts on the part of a French composer to write concerted instrumental music after the manner of Corelli. But it is his pieces for harpsichord that have brought him his greatest importance. In this, he so far outdistanced his most important predecessor, Jacques de Champion, sometimes better known as Chambonnières (1602–1672), that, though Champion composed for the harpsichord before Couperin, it is Couperin who is called the "father of French piano music."

Four volumes of Couperin's *Pièces de clavecin* represent the richest harvest produced by the early masters for the harpsichord. There is nothing quite like them—not even in Kuhnau's works—in their variety of style, their structural perfection, infinite resourcefulness of technique, aptness of musical expression, richness of atmosphere, and successful transmutation into tone of pictures, suggestions, personalities, customs, objects, incidents—in short, the successful transmutation into tone of a cross-section of French court life of the early eighteenth century.

"In composing," said Couperin in the preface of his first volume, "I have always a particular subject before my eyes. Various circumstances always suggest to me this, and also my titles." Thus his little gems are programmatic—witty, piquant, brilliant, picturesque musical depictions of butterflies, windmills, bees, roses, reapers, and so on. No one before Couperin had written so forcefully, so eloquently, so aptly for the keyboard.

If Couperin was the first French composer to affix programmatic titles to all of his pieces for the harpsichord, he was a pioneer in more significant directions as well. He was the first French composer to understand the harpsichord, and to realize its infinite potentialities. He was the first French composer to bring such a wealth of harmonic color, such an aristocratic style, such an intensity of expression, and such a fullness of lyric line to the writing of music for the harpsichord.

After Kuhnau, the most important composer of the piano sonata was Domenico Scarlatti.

Domenico Scarlatti, son of Alessandro, was born in Naples on October 26, 1685—the year which saw the birth of both Bach and Handel as well. His early mu-

sical education took place under his father. When, in
1702, Alessandro Scarlatti left Naples, Domenico was
brought to Rome where, three years later, he composed
his first opera.

He was, as his father realized only too well, endowed
with extraordinary gifts for musical creation. These
gifts, Alessandro felt strongly, must not be permitted
to be stifled. "This son of mine is an eagle whose wings
are grown. He ought not to stay idle in his nest, and
I ought not to hinder his flight." As a result, Alessandro permitted his son to travel to Venice with the
celebrated singer, Nicolini.

In Rome, where for a while he studied with Gas-
parini, he first acquired his great reputation as a virtuoso of the harpsichord. Once he entered into a "musical duel" with Handel, then visiting the city. Cardinal
Ottoboni, patron of Corelli, arranged the "match" at
his own palace. Handel and Scarlatti performed on
both the organ and the harpsichord. There were those
at his performance who insisted that Scarlatti had won
the victory on the harpsichord. But as for the organ,
Scarlatti himself graciously confessed defeat. "I have
never imagined that such organ playing was humanly
possible," he said to Handel.

As was the case of Corelli before him, and Paganini

after him, Scarlatti's phenomenal technique on the harpsichord was said by his contemporaries to have been derived from supernatural powers. "He is," they would say of him, "possessed of the devil."

In 1709, Scarlatti went to Poland to join the musical staff of the Queen. During the next few years he devoted himself to the writing of operas. In 1715, an appointment as Master of the Chapel at St. Peter's in Rome (where once the great Frescobaldi had attracted thousands of music lovers with his remarkable organ playing) brought him to the composition of church music.

But not in opera, nor in church music, did Domenico Scarlatti achieve his historic mission as a composer, but rather with the little gems for harpsichord which he called sonatas and which, likely as not, he considered as the least important of his productions.

About 1730, Domenico Scarlatti went to Spain to become the music master of the royal family, after having spent several years in London and Lisbon. There, where he lived for almost twenty-five years, he composed those little pieces for harpsichord which brought not only a new lucidity and expressiveness to writing for the keyboard but which also may be said to inaugurate the modern age of piano playing. For an altogether new technique of performance arises from the Scarlatti sonatas, a technique not even found with Couperin: runs, arpeggios, the crossing of hands—devices which brought new effects of brilliance to keyboard music.

In 1754, Domenico Scarlatti returned to Italy after his prolonged stay in Spain. Three years later he died in the city of his birth.

With Scarlatti, as with Kuhnau before him, the sonata acquired few of those traits established by Haydn in the classic form. And yet strides were made in that direction. For Scarlatti brought writing for the keyboard to such development that the major task of those who followed him was to apply this writing to the growing sonata form. He made the harpsichord speak a newer, fresher, more varied language than it had previously known. All the subtleties of musical expression were at his command: he could give voice to wit, grace, drama, a purified beauty, and always with utter enchantment. As the historian C. Hubert Parry has written:

He knows well the things that will tell, and how to awaken interest in a new mood when the effects of any particular line are exhausted. Considering how little attention had been given to technique before his time, his feats of agility are really marvelous. The variety and incisiveness of his rhythms, the peculiarities of his harmony, his wild whirling rapid passages, his rattling shakes, his leaps from end to end of the keyboard, all indicate a preternaturally vivacious temperament; and unlike many later virtuosos, he is thoroughly alive to the meaning of music as an art, and does not make his feats of dexterity his principal object. They serve as the means to convey his singularly characteristic ideas in forms as abstract as modern sonatas. The definiteness of his musical ideas is one of the most surprising things about him.

After Scarlatti, many composers produced sonatas for the harpsichord, many of them imitating the Scarlatti manner, others boldly striking for new directions on their own. Of the latter composers, one should be singled out for special discussion; for it was he who was a major figure in definitely establishing the sonata form, fashioning it with a skillful hand, making it lean, concise, practical—a pliable mould into which

Haydn and Mozart were soon to pour their inexhaustible genius.

Though the classic piano sonata was also being
formulated by the early schools in Mannheim and
Vienna, it was Karl Philipp Emanuel Bach (the greatest of the prolific brood of Johann Sebastian) who, because of his extraordinarily effective use of the sonata
form, is sometimes called its inventor. However, others
besides those in Mannheim and Vienna wrote sonatas
in a form resembling the classic before Philipp Emanuel Bach: there were his own older brother, Wilhelm
Friedemann, for example, who produced a remarkable *Sonata in D-major,* or, going back further still,
Baldassare Galuppi, the second movement of whose
Sonata in D-major forcefully presents the binary form,
a form based on two principal themes, or subjects, in
one movement.

But Karl Philipp Emanuel composed piano sonatas
with a pen as fertile as it was skilled; more than any
other composer before him he set a firm basis for the
classic piano sonata. It is only necessary to remember
that Joseph Haydn studied Philipp Emanuel Bach's sonatas long before he composed his own works in the
same form to recognize the fact that Bach remains a

significant transition between the earlier sonata of Domenico Scarlatti and the finished form achieved by the later Haydn.

Philipp Emanuel Bach was born in Weimar on March 8, 1714, to Johann Sebastian and Maria Barbara Bach. His only teacher was his father from whom he early acquired a consummate compositorial skill as well as a remarkable virtuosity in playing the harpsichord. He was an apt pupil, and his memory had unusual retentiveness: at one time he glanced over his father's shoulder at a manuscript, looked at it for a few moments, and then sat down and reproduced the entire page from memory; and at that time he was only eleven years old.

The son of Johann Sebastian Bach might be expected to be intimately in contact with music. As a boy, Philipp Emanuel often visited the Thomasschule where he heard rehearsals and performances, and rubbed elbows with the great musicians of Leipzig. And the great musicians of the outside world as well. For, as he later wrote, "no master of music passed through this place without coming to make himself known to my father and play before him."

Strange to say, Philipp Emanuel Bach was first directed by his father to law. In 1724, he was enrolled at the Thomasschule, and nine years later he was sent to Frankfort-on-the-Oder, there to complete his legal studies at the University. Music, however, was not abandoned. (As if a Bach could abandon music!) In Frankfort, Bach founded a choral society which performed several of his early works.

By 1738, Philipp Emanuel decided that music and not law was his life work. He went to Berlin, at once attracting towards his skill at the clavier the attention of the Crown Prince Frederick. When, in 1740, Frederick ascended the throne, he immediately engaged Bach as his Kapellmeister.

As Kapellmeister to Frederick the Great, Bach's duties were to accompany the flute playing of his employer (in his autobiography, Bach wrote that the first flute solo that Frederick performed as Emperor was accompanied by him), to give performances on the clavier, to compose music, and to direct musical performances. In 1744, Bach was married to Johanna Maria Danneman, the daughter of a Berlin wine merchant.

He remained many years in the court of Frederick the Great. Yet he chafed, eager for a post with fewer restrictions on his time and work. In 1767, an avenue of escape was opened to him when his godfather, the reputable Telemann, died, and Telemann's post as

Kapellmeister in Hamburg was offered to him. After much entreaty, Bach was released by the Emperor and permitted to accept the Hamburg position.

In Hamburg, Philipp Emanuel remained until the end of his life, and there he reached the height of his fame. On December 14, 1788, he died in Hamburg of pulmonary consumption.

Bach's first set of piano sonatas was published in 1742 and was dedicated to the King of Prussia. In 1744, he published the famous Württemberg sonatas. But his outstanding compositions in this form appear in a volume published in 1781, entitled *For Connoisseurs and Amateurs*. It is here that the sonata form acquired its ultimate crystallization; and it is here that a style of piano writing is evolved—the *galant* style it is called—which forms the basis of Haydn's and Mozart's piano writing. In such a miniature masterpiece as the F-minor sonata in the *Connoisseurs* collection, the first movement has achieved a definitely outlined exposition, development, and recapitulation. And a beautiful slow movement (almost in song form)—a worthy companion to Mozart's slow movements—is sandwiched between two fast ones. Thus, the three-movement sonata is definitely established by Bach, and the design of the first movement is clearly articulated. Occasionally, too (as in the F-minor sonata), there are to be found dual themes of a contrasting mood, thereby establishing the binary form as well. The sonata form was now ready for the final touches of a master; and such a master it found in Joseph Haydn.

Karl Philipp Emanuel Bach might well be called the first of the greatest masters of the piano sonata, for he was the first of them definitely to give it a distinct design, such as we know it today. From his sonatas to those of Haydn and Mozart, is only a step—not only in the structure and in the style of piano writing, but even in the freshness and charm of his melodic material and the technical fluency with which he developed his material. Both Haydn and Mozart knew the Bach sonatas well, and profited by them, as they were not slow in confessing. "For what I know, I have to thank Philipp Emanuel Bach," is the tribute of Haydn. And Mozart has said: "He is the father, and we his children. Those of us who know what is right have learned it from him; and those who have not confessed it are scoundrels."

Philipp Emanuel Bach's influence reaches even as far as Beethoven. There is something eloquently symbolic about the fact that the opening movement of

Philipp Emanuel Bach's F-minor piano sonata bears a striking resemblance to the opening movement of Beethoven's first piano sonata. It is almost as if Beethoven—beginning the composition of his first piano sonata—were consciously attempting to pay the tribute of imitation to the first master of the form. It is almost as if Beethoven wished it to be known that, now that he was to write piano sonatas, he wished to carry on where Philipp Emanuel had left off.

§ 4

LIKE the early piano sonatas of Kuhnau and Domenico Scarlatti, the earliest symphonies bear but a distant and often a hardly perceptible resemblance to the classic form crystallized by Haydn.

Actually, the word symphony—or sinfonia—was at first given by composers to any piece of music for a concerted group of instruments. Even those portions in the early operas in which the orchestra played alone (as in overtures and *ritornelli*) were referred to as sinfonias. Sinfonias appear abundantly in the Monteverdi operas. But the relationship between the early and the later symphony is not altogether a foreign one: the Italian overture of Scarlatti, also sometimes called sinfonia, consisted of three movements, two fast movements separated by a slow one.

As interest in instrumental music grew, the sinfonia became for composers a medium quite apart from sheer incidental passages in operas. They exploited it, beginning to write music exclusively for orchestral groups, which were to be performed independently. But these earliest sinfonias were inchoate in form, without coherence or direction; and the composers were almost always at a loss to produce a style that lent itself to instrumental performance.

The permanent establishment of the symphony as a form for instrumental music (in short, a large work in three movements, based upon the laws of variety and contrast) is largely the distinction of a composer from Mannheim, Johann Stamitz, upon whose shoulders, as Hugo Riemann wrote, rest Haydn and Mozart.[1]

It is hardly possible to overestimate Stamitz's historic importance. He was like Monteverdi, Gluck, Pergolesi and Corelli, a far-visioned pioneer, breaking the hard ground and fertilizing it with new seed. Before Stamitz, instrumental music had been composed by such early masters as Corelli, Sammartini (himself a composer of some twenty symphonies), Vivaldi. Inevitably, Stamitz learned more than one lesson about form, thematic construction, and instrumental style

[1] However, as is proved in a somewhat later section, no less important than Stamitz in establishing the symphony as a form for instrumental music was the early Viennese school which was functioning coincidentally with Stamitz.

from the early sonata and concerto grosso. But more clearly than anyone before him—much more clearly than Sammartini, for example, whose symphonies are little more than extended sinfonias—Stamitz saw the shape that the symphony must assume if it was to achieve structural unity, balance, and contrast. With composers like Sammartini, the symphony was hardly more than an embryo in form, without distinguishable features. Instrumentation was a comparatively unknown art. Symphonic structure was yet an unexplored science. Even a standardized orchestra was lacking, for composers like Sammartini wrote for any combination of instruments, almost casually arrived at.

But, without much precedent to guide him, Stamitz was one of the first to establish a new form, to solidify its foundations and to erect a majestic structure which required only the minor finishing touches of his successors before it could become the sanctuary of the genius of Haydn and Mozart. And Stamitz brought into being what for his period could be considered a wonderfully balanced orchestra, capable of giving full expression to his symphonic ideas. It is Stamitz, therefore —even more than Haydn—who deserves to be considered the father of the modern symphony.

[*171*]

PIONEERS IN MUSIC

Johann Wenzel Anton Stamitz was born in Deutsch-brod, Bohemia, on June 19, 1717. His early music study brought him to the violin on which he acquired considerable virtuosity. His career can be said to have begun in his twenty-fifth year when he became solo violinist for the coronation festivities of Emperor Karl VII of Frankfurt. This performance attracted the attention of Elector Palatine Karl Theodor who, one year later, engaged Stamitz as his chamber musician. Thus Stamitz was brought to Mannheim, the city where he reached world fame as a conductor and composer and where he founded the Mannheim orchestra which was responsible for the development of the modern symphony orchestra and the birth of the modern symphony.

In 1745, Stamitz became concertmaster and conductor of the Mannheim orchestra. In this position he made history. He may well be said to have been one of the first important conductors, since he was one of the first to lay stress on the preparation of a musical work before performance and to demand the most rigid discipline from his men. He may also be said to have created the first modern symphony orchestra. He developed his orchestra into a technical instrument unique at the time. He explored, for the first time, such dynamic resources of orchestral playing as *crescendo* and *diminuendo,* and amazed his contemporaries with the unanimity and decisiveness with which the orchestral players performed these effects. The historian Burney said of this Mannheim symphonic ensemble:

> No orchestra in the world has ever surpassed the Mannheim orchestra in execution. Its *forte* is thunder, its *crescendo* is cataract, its *diminuendo* is a crystal stream babbling along in the distance, its *piano* a breath of spring.

He added that it was a "band of generals." Young Mozart, too, is known to have heard the Mannheim orchestra and to have spoken his praises in vocabulary no less glowing.

Stamitz brought his orchestra from Mannheim to the rest of Europe in an extensive concert tour. Wherever he went he amazed his audiences with the virtuosity of his men.

It is not superfluous to point out Stamitz's pioneer significance in creating such a modern orchestral instrument; for the birth of the modern orchestra and the modern symphony went hand in hand. The orchestra he conducted was composed of between forty and fifty men, well coördinated and well balanced in the variety of its instruments. There were twenty violins (ten firsts and ten seconds); four violas and four violoncellos; two basses, flutes, oboes, horns, and bassoons; also a trumpet and a kettledrum. In composing his symphonies, Stamitz had in mind a model orchestra, the same orchestra which (with certain amplifications, particularly in the reed section) Haydn and Mozart employed. In this, if in nothing else, Stamitz struck the note of modernity in his employment of a well-adjusted instrumentation for his music. But in other respects as well. A meticulous conductor, Stamitz was equally painstaking about orchestral balance, subtlety of phrasing and the pronunciation of an inherently instrumental language when he composed music for an orchestral body.

Stamitz composed about fifty symphonies which are among the first significant works in this most significant of all musical forms. The new homophonic style achieves greater emancipation than ever. Subtlety of dynamics appears for the first time. But more important still is the fact that with Stamitz the symphony form emerges from behind its former distorting haze. The first movement acquires with Stamitz even greater clarity of design than it had previously known: Sym-

phonies like the fifth one in Opus 9 have a first movement in which the binary form is once and for all
established, the two themes of a contrasting nature
being forcefully stated, then developed, and finally repeated. The Stamitz symphony, generally in three
movements, occasionally bears a close similarity to a
similar work by Haydn. Symphonies by Stamitz like
one in D-major employed four movements: The first
was in a large mould, bigger in scope and design than
any of the others; the second was lyrical, like an aria;
the third movement comprised a minuet and trio; and
the fourth was a vivacious and deft fast movement.
Never before this, had the modern symphony been so
clearly defined.

Romain Rolland goes so far as to say that,

> the roots of Beethoven already exist . . . in the
> Mannheim symphonies, in the work of that as-
> tonishing Johann Stamitz. . . . Through him,
> instrumental music becomes the supple gar-
> ment of the living soul, always in movement,
> perpetually changing, with its unexpected fluc-
> tuations and changes. . . . I have no hesitancy
> in saying that the symphonies of Stamitz, though
> less rich, less beautiful, less exuberant, are much

more spontaneous than those of a Haydn or a
Mozart. It is made to its own measure; it creates
its own forms; it does not submit to them.

The last comment is well worth underscoring: the
Stamitz symphony, at its best, never submitted to its
form. Of the early composers of the symphony, he is
one of the rare creators who does not become stylized
and does not imitate himself repetitiously. The best
of Stamitz's symphonies can be a perpetual joy even
to discriminating twentieth century music lovers, and
it is to be greatly regretted that they are not more fully
exploited by present-day conductors.

But the first symphonies of Haydn owe an equally
great debt to the Viennese style of instrumental music
which was undergoing subtle evolution, growth, and
change for many years before Haydn's time. The Viennese period in music is, with no little justification, accepted by the historian as the most productive epoch
in the history of music. A school of music which
produced Haydn and Mozart (and somewhat later
Beethoven and Schubert), which saw the full enrichment of the symphony, the sonata, the quartet, as well
as the birth of the *Lied,* certainly can stand within
the pages of musical history without a rival.

[*176*]

But just as the Haydn symphonies owe their structure and design to Stamitz, so they owe their graceful, charming fluent style to the early years of music-making in Vienna.

It is, therefore, strange to remark that the early history of Viennese music (that is to say music in Vienna before Haydn) is a subject generally ignored by the historian. Even the eminent Sir William H. Hadow, in his volume on the Viennese period in the *Oxford History of Music,* made little effort to trace the spiritual and stylistic heritage which the Viennese masters of the late eighteenth and early nineteenth centuries received from their predecessors. Yet this heritage serves to explain the emergence of the magnificent Viennese period, beginning with Haydn. More than that, this heritage discloses the original source of the famous Viennese style of musical composition—the identifying fingerprints on the music of almost every Viennese composer from Haydn up to the World War.

When, in 1736, Gluck first came to Vienna and was received by the patron's hospitality of Prince Lobkowitz, Vienna was already a great city of music. The Emperor, Charles VI (himself a distinguished performer on the clavichord) spent annually some two

[*177*]

hundred thousand gulden to maintain the court orchestra and opera—an unheard-of extravagance at the
time! The noblemen of Vienna, always taking their
cue from the Emperor, were equally lavish in their
expenditures for music. Prince Lobkowitz, for example, had his own orchestra, a whole retinue of singers,
actors, and musicians. Almost at any hour of the day,
rehearsals of musical works took place at the Lobkowitz palace; and often, several at a time in different
parts of the house.

Yet, as Gluck learned when he became more intimately associated with Vienna's musical life, though
there was an efflorescence of musical activity in Vienna,
the city was at the same time sterile creatively. Musically speaking, Vienna was but a colony of the Italians.
The generosity of the Court had brought to it the great
art of the Italians, which was then in great vogue
among the Viennese patrons. The court poet was an
Italian—Metastasio; the imperial chamber composer
and assistant Kapellmeister, Antonio Caldara, was also
an Italian. Rarely—all too rarely!—the work of a German composer was performed—say, an opera by Johann Adolph Hasse or Reinhard Keiser. But the taste
of the time reacted most strongly to Italian art. Most
generally, it was an opera of Scarlatti, Marcello Du-

rante, Sammartini that was heard and admired in the famous palaces of Vienna.

Of music by native Austrian composers there was a poverty. The popularity of an Austrian composer was dependent entirely on his ability to adapt himself to the Italian style. For example, Johann Joseph Fux, Kapellmeister to Charles VI . . .

Johann Joseph Fux was born in Styria of peasant stock in 1660. He came to Vienna in his youth, became an organist at the *Zu den Schotten,* and married a Viennese woman. In 1698 he was appointed court composer, and then until 1718 he served at St. Stephen's church as Kapellmeister. In 1718, he resigned his position at the Church to become the Kapellmeister of the Emperor.

Undoubtedly, Fux owed his exalted station—and the frequency with which his music was performed—to the fact that though he was Austrian by birth he conscientiously followed the lead of the popular Italian composers of the time. His most famous opera, *Costanza e Fortezza,* imitates the ornamental vocal decorations of Alessandro Scarlatti, as well as Scarlatti's Italian overture and the use of both the *da capo* aria and the accompanied recitative. His sonatas, sinfonias, and overtures imitated Corelli's contrapuntal chamber sonatas. But Fux could never completely conform to the Italian style. To his assumed Italian lyric line and Italian clarity of instrumental writing there clung a German pedantry. Spontaneity and freshness of spirit are rarely found in Fux's music. His is, essentially, the work of a careful and well-disciplined schoolmaster. His church music reveals a skillful polyphonic hand, particularly when he writes for three voices; but of imagination or originality there is not much. His instrumental writing is formulistic and without inspiration. Skill he had; but not genius. It is uniquely appropriate that the only one of Fux's works to survive him is his book of exercises, the *Gradus ad Parnassum*.

Despite his important position at court, Fux was never a great favorite of the Viennese. They considered him too rhetorical and cold. They much preferred Antonio Caldara, the composer-of-the-hour in Vienna, whose enormous popularity was but another indication of the Italian tastes prevailing in Vienna at the time. Where Fux was learned, Caldara was simple, forthright, unpretentious; where Fux was self-conscious and even stilted, Caldara was clear and fresh.

Caldara's background was Italian, and his style was in the best Italian traditions, though it did strive for a great simplicity of structure. From his master, Legrenzi, Caldara learned how to write arias with mobility and ease; how to give his music clarity; how to write opera buffa with a good-humored pen. Less meretricious in his melodic writing than the Italian masters, he was often much more touching and tender.

Caldara first came to Vienna in 1712, in his forty-second year. Behind him lay a successful career as opera composer, and as a virtuoso on the violoncello. After a short trip to Madrid, he returned to Vienna and remained there for the rest of his life, serving as second Kapellmeister to Fux. Vienna took to Caldara as it could never quite take to Fux.

Caldara wrote many choral and instrumental works, but his best music was operatic. Even his instrumental works are more vocal in the juxtaposition of lyric line and accompaniment; and his church cantatas are operatic in the dramatic fire of the recitative and the lyrical flow of the aria.[1]

On February 13, 1736, Caldara's opera, *Achille in Sciro* was performed to celebrate the wedding of Maria Theresa to the Duke of Lorraine. If Gluck was then in Vienna (the exact date of his arrival is unknown) he most certainly attended a performance which was

[1] For example, *La Rosa* and *Che prodigio* in vol. 75 of the *Denkmäler der Tonkunst in Österreich.*

the most festive musical event in Vienna at the time. At any rate, Gluck had sufficient opportunity to hear other Caldara operas that year: *Ciro riconosciuto* performed on August 28, and *Temistocle* presented ten weeks later on the name-day of Charles VI. For Caldara, Gluck expressed warm admiration; his enthusiasm for Caldara's aristocratic vocal style was no less genuine than that of the princely patrons of Vienna.

Gluck did not remain long in Vienna. We have already seen that he left on a long journey with Prince Melzi, from which he was not to return to Vienna until 1748, after an absence of twelve years. He was no longer the young composer seeking his fortune when he returned to Vienna, but a composer with well-established fame.

Musical life in Vienna had undergone great change during the twelve years of Gluck's absence. For a time, an appalling decay had set in. Caldara had died in 1736, and Fux in 1741. No composer of comparable stature had arisen in their places.

Austria, moreover, was beset by political struggles which smothered all musical activity. In 1740, Charles VI died, and was succeeded by Maria Theresa. With the ascension of Frederick the Great in Prussia, the

Silesian Wars began—wars in which Austria was disastrously involved. For a while it seemed that defeats abroad and dissensions at home (Maria Theresa's right to the throne was seriously questioned) would bring her reign to an abrupt end. Only the personal magnetism of the Empress, her strength of will, her resourcefulness and tact saved her throne—and, possibly, the Empire. She acquired important allies, and formidable foreign loans. She inspired her soldiers with excess patriotism on the battlefield. Soon there were victories; and each victory further solidified the position of the Empress. By 1748, Austria knew partial peace and a return of prosperity. And it enjoyed greater dignity in Europe than ever before.

The first few years of Maria Theresa's reign, weighed down as they were by ponderous problems of state, saw a disintegration of Vienna's musical forces. Maria Theresa, a remarkable musician in her own right, had little patience with musical entertainment. Performances at court had, for a while, virtually ceased to exist.

But the return of political stability had brought to Vienna a renascence of its musical life. Shortly before 1748, Vienna was once again a center of music-making. Private opera companies and private orchestras were once again industriously making music in the many palaces; and Kapellmeisters were busily engaged in producing new works for these performances. There was now even a new opera house, the Burgtheater, for the public performances of opera. The Burgtheater had opened in 1741 and suffered during the next few years, as all musical organizations did in Vienna. It closed down. Then, with a change of directorial hands, it reopened in 1748 with a new lease on life.

The most significant musical change in Vienna was not the renewal of musical activity. More momentous, by far, was the emergence of a group of pioneer composers—many of them Viennese by birth—who attempted to turn away from the Italian style and to write in their own vein. Not that the Italian manner was discredited in Vienna! The great success of Niccolò Jommelli and his *Didone,* in 1748, was emphatic proof that Vienna still preferred the Italian way of writing music. But, in spite of the preferences of the Viennese, a group of composers was bravely refusing to ape the Italian composers. These Viennese composers were producing music supple in construction, graceful in style, music full of charm and buoyancy. This music was the first perceptible sign of a Viennese style of composition, different from the Italian and the German. This music, in short, was the foundation upon which the later period of Haydn and Mozart was to be erected.

Principal among these new composers was Georg Matthias Monn, who must be considered the first important Viennese composer. Actually, the Viennese Period began with him. He was born in Vienna in 1717, and died there in 1750. He was the organist at the Karlskirche. His most productive years came after 1740, particularly in the closing years of the decade when he created his best symphonies, trio-sonatas, and quartet-fugues.

Monn was the first composer in Austria to employ the "new" instrumental style out of which grew the modern symphony, the "new" style so successfully employed by Johann Stamitz in Mannheim. There are some musicologists who believe that it is Monn, and not Stamitz, who was its father; but that remains a questionable point. In any case, it was Monn who introduced the style to Vienna, where it was to achieve such wonderful development. Even in his early symphonies—one in D-major, composed in 1740, is a good case in point—there is the use of light and shade for contrast of mood; a first movement in binary form with a clearly suggested exposition, development and recapitulation can be found; there is a second movement of a lyrical nature, but instrumental rather than vocal in quality, and a third movement, minuet in form. In Monn's later symphonies, the form is even more clearly defined, the style is purified, the ideas elevated in tone.

Whether it was Monn or Stamitz who was the first perpetrator of the new instrumental style is a subject of fascination for the musicologist; it need not concern us here. What is important for us is the fact that, independent of Stamitz in Mannheim, Monn was pioneering on virgin soil. And it is important for us to notice that there are differences as well as similarities in the music of Stamitz and Monn. Structurally, a symphony by Stamitz (one in D-major for example) and one by Monn are similar. But the language of each composer is radically different. Stamitz has greater robustness; Monn, greater deftness and grace. The melodic material of Stamitz is of stronger fiber; Monn often achieves extreme delicacy. Already there is perceptible in Monn a style of composition that is Viennese, different in mood and temperament from the music produced by the neighboring Germans.[1]

---

[1] The modern composer, Arnold Schönberg, has adapted and edited a concerto for violoncello by Monn.

Like Monn, Giuseppe Bonno was Viennese by birth; like Monn, his music has a fluid style, good taste and instinct. Bonno was born in 1710, the son of the imperial running footman. His talent attracted the attention of the Emperor who sent him to Naples to study music. In 1738, Bonno was accepted in the Imperial Chapel of Vienna as *Hofscholar*. One year later, he received an appointment as *Hofcompositeur* of the Imperial Chapel.

Bonno's compositions played an important part in Viennese musical life after 1745. His oratorios were performed each year after Lent at the Imperial Chapel, and his *festi teatrali,* or "occasional cantatas," were frequently presented before the royal archduchesses and their imperial parents at the Court.

But Bonno did not confine his creative gifts entirely to choral music, but wrote voluminously for instruments: serenatas, pastorales, symphonies—all of considerable charm. Mozart knew Bonno's music and admired it greatly; and when one studies the consummate taste that went into the construction of a Bonno symphony one can well understand why. At a performance of one of Bonno's symphonies, Mozart reverently referred to the composer as *der alte ehrliche brave Mann* ("the old, honest, gallant man").

PIONEERS IN MUSIC

Christoph Wagenseil, a pupil of Fux, was the court composer and personal music master of Maria Theresa and the imperial princesses. He was born in Vienna in 1715, and died there in 1777. His master, Fux, recommended him for a court scholarship in 1736, and for a post as court composer in 1739.

Wagenseil was not a great composer, nor a particularly original one. A symphony in D-major, composed in 1746, is beautifully realized; but the ideas are trite. Other later instrumental works—sonatas as well as symphonies—have a transparency of writing, and a bright-faced sparkle. But his music is, for the most part, a manufactured item; it has neither the personality of a symphony of Monn nor the individuality of one by Bonno. Essentially, Wagenseil's role was a subsidiary one in the evolution of Viennese music.

It was a harpsichord concerto by Wagenseil that the *Wunderkind* Mozart performed at the Schönbrunn palace in 1762, with the composer himself standing nearby, agape with wonder.

Florian Leopold Gassmann, like Wagenseil a composer of smaller stature, had also the redeeming gift of grace and tasteful technique. An opera buffa, *La Contessina,* is a gem of iridescence, of freshness of spirit, of lustre of wit. Its sinfonia is a perfect example of Vi-

[*188*]

ennese symphonic writing before Haydn, in the exquisite elegance of the form. Notice, even, how Mozartean is the fleeting grace of the closing section of the
third movement! A symphony in B-minor is also unusual for the buoyancy and zest of its spirit. Gassmann
was, obviously, at his best in writing in the lighter vein.
The Viennese style acquired in his music greater elucci-
dation.

Gassmann was born in Brux in 1729 and died in
Vienna in 1774. His musical apprenticeship took place
in Italy, where he first achieved success. In 1762, he
arrived in Vienna, becoming court Kapellmeister six
years later. Gassmann died accidentally by falling out
of his carriage.

Two other composers whose writings suggested a
Viennese personality were Josef Starzer (1726–1787)
and Johann Christoph Mann (1726–1782). But such
of their music as I have seen has very little genuine distinction, other than an essential fluency and a certain
charm.

But grace and charm, buoyancy and lightness of
touch are not the only characteristics of the Viennese
style perfected and enriched by Haydn and Mozart.
More important still is the felicitousness of musical ex-

pression—the choice of the exact idea, and the mould-
ing of it into the exact form it demands; the exquisite
sense for architectonic construction; a consummate
skill in carving thematic material into a perfectly balanced tonal design; freshness, youth, wit and deep
feeling.

Such qualities are sometimes suggested in the symphonies of Ignaz Pleyel (1757–1831) and Leopold Hoff-
mann (1730–1793); but they achieve their fullest realization in the earlier symphonies and quartets of Karl
von Dittersdorf.

The paradox of Karl von Dittersdorf is that he was
too greatly appreciated in his own time, and too little
in ours. He was, most assuredly, not the greatest composer of his day, as so many in Vienna acclaimed him
at the height of his career—an amazing estimation
when one recalls that he was a contemporary of Haydn
and Mozart. But, on the other hand, Dittersdorf little
deserves the neglect which has been his fate ever since
his own day. If he is not a Haydn or a Mozart, he is
nevertheless a composer of formidable gifts. If he did
not possess the extraordinary inventiveness and profound depths of his two famous contemporaries, he
possessed other qualities which should bring him a
position of importance among the minor composers in

history. Dittersdorf's music, at its best, has too much taste and imagination, too much charm, to deserve the silence of a full century.

His symphonies, concertos, and quartets frequently disclose remarkable pages of music—remarkable particularly when it is recalled that the earliest of these were composed before Haydn reached maturity as a composer. Even as early as 1766, his symphonies (one in C-major is an excellent example) show an extraordinary feeling for the symphonic form, a daring in the use of musical transitions, and a rich harmonic and rhythmic language. His slow sections have grace of movement, flexibility of design, and warmth of feeling, such as is found in the best of Haydn's works. Dittersdorf's early quartets are striking examples of homophonic writing for four voices, in which, for the first time, the four voices are given equal importance, and in which can be found a style that is always transparent in texture, and graceful. He brought to the quartet coherence of form and refinement of style, and in doing so he prepared it for Haydn.

Though he never achieved in his later music that increased richness of expression, that moving feeling, and that nobility of thought which would have made him an immortal together with Haydn and Mozart, he was always a composer inexhaustible in his charm, extraordinary in technique, and varied in the mood of his music. More than that, too, a quartet in A-major, the sixth of a set of six, shows a boldness of execution, harmonic progressions that are new and rich, striking rhythmic figures, and an ability to expand the rigid outlines of the then-existing forms which are nothing short of extraordinary for a composer who lived in the middle of the eighteenth century.

Dittersdorf's tragedy was that he lived at a time when Haydn and Mozart were at the height of their powers, and was not of their creative stature. In any other age, Dittersdorf would have been acclaimed a master, and his music would have come down to us as an important contribution of a great and original composer.

He was born as Karl Ditters on November 2, 1739, in Vienna, where his father was an embroiderer by trade. Sensitive to music, Karl was given by his father a good musical training from early childhood. Karl was a good student, and while still a boy received employment as violinist in St. Stephen's church. There his talent attracted the attention of a horn player who, in turn, recommended him highly to that eminent Viennese patron, Prince von Hildburghausen. In his eleventh year, Karl Ditters became the page-boy to the Prince, who saw to it that he received competent instruction in music, languages, and the social graces.

When financial difficulties compelled the Prince to disband his orchestra in 1761, Ditters became a violinist in the Imperial Chapel, where life proved difficult, indeed, for the young musician. The work was hard; the pay, poor. However, at this time, Ditters met and became a friend of Gluck—then, already, a person of considerable consequence in Vienna. Through Gluck's influence, the work at the Chapel was decreased for young Ditters, and an additional income was made possible to him through the assumption of some private pupils in music. The friendship between Gluck and Ditters soon became so intimate that at one time Gluck urged the younger man to make a concert tour with him through Italy. Ditters, of course, accepted—and made several successful appearances as violinist.

His first important employment was as Kapellmeister to the Bishop of Grosswardein, in Pressburg, Hungary, a post which Ditters accepted in 1764. Here, Ditters directed weekly concerts, and for these concerts he composed many oratorios, symphonies and quartets which were later to make him famous.

Those were happy years for Ditters, who now knew comfort and peace as well as artistic satisfaction. It was, however, not destined to continue for a long time. In 1769, rumors of scandalous living at Grosswardein reached the ears of Maria Theresa who vigorously reprimanded the Bishop. As partial atonement, the Bishop decided to disband his orchestra.

Ditters' next position, as Kapellmeister to Count Schaffgotsch, the Prince Bishop of Breslau, was even more desirable. Life at the Count's estates in Johannisberg in Prussian Silesia became for Ditters soft and luxurious—increasingly so, as Ditters became more and more of a personal friend to the Count. The Count heaped honors upon his favorite musician and friend: first, the Order of the Golden Spur; then, the post of Overseer of Forests; finally, the position of Chief Magistrate, which brought with it the patent of nobility.

His name was now Karl von Dittersdorf. He was now a nobleman, and he took to nobility as though he had been born in high station. He became excessively vain, fond of pomp, ceremony, and outward display. Lavish dress, sumptuous settings, luxury, and softness became indispensable to him.

But luxury and a soft life did not mar his musical production. He composed in every form, and his music grew increasingly popular—particularly in Vienna where it soon became something of a vogue. In 1773, Karl von Dittersdorf visited Vienna to assist at a performance of his oratorio, *Esther*. He was given a regal welcome, and was acclaimed with almost delirious enthusiasm. Emperor Joseph II offered him the post of Kapellmeister at his court—the highest musical position in Vienna. But Dittersdorf refused, only because the leisure and comforts of Johannisberg meant too much to him.

The success of *Esther* in Vienna was great, but no greater than that of his other works. He appeared in the Augarten in performances of his own concertos and symphonies, and met acclaim. His opera, *The Doctor and the Apothecary*, received such a rousing reception that Dittersdorf was immediately commissioned to compose three more operas in a similar style. Dittersdorf's symphonies, quartets, and concertos were performed frequently in the leading Viennese palaces. They called him the greatest composer of the age, as if oblivious of the fact that Haydn and Mozart were at that very time creating masterpieces.

But Dittersdorf soon paid the price of this exaggerated acclaim; reaction set in inevitably. And the reaction left him a forgotten composer. When his friend, the Count, died, Dittersdorf lost his sinecure and was given a meager pension. No other position was open to him. Even in Vienna, they seemed to have forgotten that they had once worshiped him. But for the fact that a music patron, Count Still, took the composer to his own home to take care of him, Dittersdorf might well have known starvation.

Such closing years were bleak to a man who had received the greatest riches of life—recognition, fame, wealth, adoration. Dittersdorf was forced to realize that his day had ended, that he was a forgotten composer. His importance had become so deflated that, at one time, Breitkopf and Härtel, the publishers, were forced to tell him that they could no longer publish any more of his works because there no longer existed a demand.

In bitterness, Dittersdorf dictated his autobiography, his last testament to a fickle world. Brokenhearted by his fate, Dittersdorf died in Bohemia on October 24, 1799.

Fate hardly proved kinder to Dittersdorf after his death. He remained the forgotten composer, a composer too highly praised in his own day, too little known after it. Occasionally, a string quartet of his is revived by an adventurous chamber music ensemble, and at such times the sparkle and brilliance of his music, and the independence of his thinking amaze critics who come expecting to hear a museum piece. But, except for occasional and infrequent performances of a quartet, Dittersdorf's music remains unknown to us.

In 1761, Joseph Haydn entered the service of Prince Esterházy at Eisenstadt. He had already composed his first string quartet and his first symphony. But his complete unfoldment in both these departments—his emergence as the first of the undisputed masters of the symphony and quartet—was yet to take place.

In 1781, Mozart settled permanently in Vienna. He had, of course, already been a rich creative force, and the author of many masterpieces. But his richest, profoundest vein—and the culmination of his style—did not assert itself until Vienna where he came into contact with Haydn and was influenced by him.

With Haydn and Mozart the Viennese Period was in flower. Beethoven (who settled in Vienna in 1792) and Franz Schubert (who composed his first masterpiece, *Gretchen am Spinnrade* in 1814) were to bring this period still greater riches, and still newer worlds of beauty.

But the Viennese Period had not begun with Haydn.

When Haydn brought his inspiration, taste, his warm sense of humor, exquisite sense of style, endless imagination, and independence to the symphony and the string quartet, the stage had been set for him. Haydn brought to successful realization the pioneer work of lesser and forgotten masters; and it is they who made his emergence possible.

III

A FEW MUSICAL FORMS

John Field

Johann Strauss (the father)

Josef Lanner

Franz Liszt

§ 1

BEFORE Johann Sebastian Bach there were Carissimi and Buxtehude. Monteverdi and Gluck preceded Wagner; and Haydn and Mozart developed out of Stamitz, the early Viennese school and Philipp Emanuel Bach.

In much the same manner, Frédéric Chopin was evolved out of John Field.

John Field—the name is hardly known to the average music lover; his works, even less so. Yet he belongs to that noble lineage of composers for the piano which began with Kuhnau, Couperin, and Domenico Scarlatti. That lineage was ultimately to produce a Chopin. And in the production of Chopin, John Field was to play a major role.

The historian recognizes Field as the inventor of a brief but exquisite form for the piano which was picturesquely entitled by the composer a nocturne. This form Field bequeathed to Chopin, a fact which alone would have earned for Field the gratitude of the music world. Yet Field went even further, for as Franz Liszt pointed out—and who could be a better judge? —Field's pieces for the piano "clear the way for all subsequent efforts appearing under the names of Songs Without Words, impromptus,[1] ballades and the like." In short, John Field was one of the sources—possibly the most important—out of which has coursed the romantic literature for the piano.

To study John Field's piano music is to recognize forcefully that he anticipated the pulse and heart-beat of Chopin. Chopin's enchanting chromaticism, Chopin's full and warm romantic singing, Chopin's remarkable elasticity of form, even something of Chopin's extraordinary knowledge of the resources of his instrument are qualities which are found to a degree in the best of Field's piano works. Field was, probably, the first of the Romantic composers for the piano. His influence on the development of piano music was of inestimable importance. Yet he was not only a pioneer but a formidable creator in his own right. At his best, Field possessed a personal speech that combined tenderness and melancholy, sweetness and pain—all expressed in accents of unforgettable beauty. His pieces—of in-

[1] The famous Schubert impromptus were not thus entitled by him.

comparable perfection in form and appropriateness of musical expression—are (as the English critic, Ernest Walker, once wrote) "exquisite polished miniatures, with their delicate melodies and their shy, fugitive gracefulness."

John Field was born in Dublin, Ireland, on July 26, 1782—nine years before the death of Mozart. Field's unusual talent for music revealed itself early. His father, a violinist in a Dublin theatre, arranged to have John study the piano. Unfortunately, John Field's grandfather (no doubt inspired with visions of a magnificent concert career for his grandson; for the memory of the triumphs of the *Wunderkind* Mozart were still fresh in mind) decided to superintend these piano studies personally. With a ruthless hand that was not reluctant to inflict heavy blows of punishment, the grandfather supervised John Field's piano studies. In this way, Field was officially introduced to music. It is fortunate that the boy's enthusiasm for music was so great that not even severe blows and the iron hand of discipline could stifle it.

Field, however, was soon freed from his grandfather's tyranny. He was placed with Tommaso, a well-known piano teacher in Dublin. Tommaso's sympathetic understanding and his warm affection—striking contrasts to what Field had experienced until now!—inspired new enthusiasm in the boy. He now made swift progress. In his tenth year he was able to make his first public appearance at the Spiritual Concerts in Dublin which were directed by Giordani. This appearance met with such enthusiasm that two more concerts followed; and at one of these Field introduced his first composition, a *Rondo.*

In his twelfth year, John Field—already the proud possessor of an enviable reputation as a prodigy—was brought to London by his father, who had been engaged for the orchestra in the Haymarket Theatre. While here, his father met Clementi, the well-known pianist and composer who had turned to the manufacture of pianos. Clementi deeply interested himself in young Field and offered to give him regular instruction if, in return, he would become his apprentice and work in the warehouse. It was a fair exchange. Field worked for Clementi, and studied under him. He adapted himself to the eccentricities of his master (Clementi's greatest fault was his excessive thriftiness), and catered to them. In return, Field profited immeasurably from the valuable advice and teachings of one of the foremost living authorities of the piano.

In his first appearances as pianist in London, in the spring of 1794, Field revealed a growing maturity, and before long he enjoyed a formidable reputation as a virtuoso. And as a composer, as well—for, in 1799, John Field introduced his first piano concerto at the Pinto Concerts, and its fluidity of musical writing as well as the warm emotion of its ideas aroused considerable praise.

Notwithstanding Field's mounting prestige both as a pianist and composer, he remained an apprentice to Clementi for many years. A close bond of friendship developed between teacher and pupil. Clementi was only too well aware of Field's extraordinary musical gifts, and was prepared at all times to give him assistance in furthering his artistic career. In 1801, Clementi (who watched his pence so scrupulously that he did his own laundry!) furnished the funds for the publication of Field's *Three Sonatas*, the first of Field's published works. One year later, he accompanied his protégé on an extensive concert tour which brought them to Paris, Vienna, and as far as St. Petersburg; and wherever Field performed he was received with acclaim.

When, in 1803, Clementi made preparations to return from Russia to England, Field decided that he would settle permanently in St. Petersburg. He liked

Russia, and he had already established himself among the Russians as one of the most celebrated pianists of the time. As Glinka, the great Russian nationalist composer who became Field's pupil in 1814, wrote some years later:

> Field's playing was at once sweet and strong and characterized by admirable precision. His fingers fell on the keys as large drops of rain that spread themselves like iridescent pearls.

With permanent residence in St. Petersburg, Field's prestige as a musician soared and swelled. His name became something of a household word, and to become his pupil was the highest aspiration of every young music student in highest society. Inevitably, Field amassed a fortune, and innumerable honors beat a path to his door.

He now became very much of a *grand homme*. Luxury and display appealed to him, and he adopted them. He acquired a sumptuous home, four dogs, several carriages, and the finest of clothing. He overindulged in food and drink, which not only brought on physical flabbiness but also mental indolence. He assumed the airs of a gracious patron: each Sunday morning he held

open house for all those who were in need and dis-
tributed five rubles to each one.

Wealth and fame and self-pampering brought on his
artistic ruin. In the early years of his Russian sojourn,
he composed works like the *Piano Quintet* and a new
piano concerto which revealed his growing powers as
a creator in the larger musical forms. With soft living,
however, came a stifling reluctance to do any work. In
1808, he married a French actress, and their marriage
was unhappy from the very first (they were separated in
1813); domestic problems made hard work even less
possible.

Yet he was able to turn to composition from time to
time, and in place of large works he composed small
pieces of incomparable charm and perfection. In 1814,
he composed the first of his nocturnes—the first time
that such a name appeared on a musical composition,
the forerunner of the form which Chopin was to fill
with such a wealth of poetry.

It would, however, be a sad understatement to speak
of Field's nocturnes merely as the forerunners of those
by Chopin. In his most felicitous expressions in this
form (the fourth nocturne in A-major is an eloquent
example) he achieved Chopinesque delicacy, poignancy,
and tenderness with unerring fingers. He, too, was a

[*207*]

poet. He, too, could mould tones into exquisite miniatures. He could be as sensitive in his choice of the
lyric phrase, as varied in his use of nuance, as brilliant in his effects as Chopin. Johann Rellstab goes so
far as to place the Field nocturnes on a higher artistic
plane than those of Chopin. And the modern English
critic, Eric Blom, echoes such a judgment when he
writes:

> Field is unique. . . . There is nothing else
> to take their place, not even Chopin's similarly
> named pieces. Here, he sings his heart out, and
> it is because he has learnt to sing that he be-
> comes so entirely himself. . . . His range of
> mood within the species of the nocturne is ex-
> traordinary—far greater than Chopin's. . . .
> [Here] John Field gave something to the world
> of music without which it would be as the world
> of flowers without the daisy; no worse for those
> who do not know what they miss, but not free
> from wistful regret for those who had once be-
> held the modest blossom.

While Franz Liszt makes no attempt to compare the
respective merits of Field and Chopin, he grows no
less lyrical when he contemplates Field's nocturnes.

Their tones, already, transport us into those hours when the soul, freed from the burden of the day and resting only in itself, soars upward to the mysterious regions of the starry heights.

In 1822, Field changed his home from St. Petersburg to Moscow, where more than ever he became a victim to his vices: the love for luxury, indolence, self-indulgence. His life was being wasted with idleness and dissipation. He took to drink as never before; and more than ever composition became a rare occupation. He now even began to neglect his piano playing and his teaching engagements. Such a life was not only to bring disintegration to Field's spirit and to his creative powers but to his financial income as well. It was not long before both poverty and ill-health claimed him.

By 1832 his life had become sordid. He had squandered his savings, lost his income, even dissipated his own self-respect. In an attempt to rouse himself from his squalor, he decided to abandon Russia and to return to England—after an absence of thirty years. He was given a welcome accorded to kings. His performance of his own E-flat concerto, with the Royal Philharmonic Orchestra, was an occasion for wild enthusiasm. These triumphs succeeded, at least partially, in restoring something of his one-time self-esteem.

One month after his return to London, his friend, teacher and patron—Muzio Clementi—passed away. Field was one of his chief mourners at the funeral services at Westminster Abbey.

Following his London successes, Field began an extensive concert tour throughout Europe. In Paris, he had an opportunity of hearing Chopin for the first time. It cannot be said that Field recognized Chopin's genius, or even discerned that in Chopin he could find a kindred creative spirit. From Paris, Field went on to Brussels, then to Switzerland, and Italy. It was a march of triumph. It seemed that Field was on his way to a new and greater career as a musician.

However, his earlier follies had left their marks upon him. In May of 1834, he fell seriously ill in Naples. He was brought to a hospital for a serious operation and for many months he hovered between life and death. When, finally, recovery enabled him to leave the hospital, he was penniless. It was fortunate, indeed, that he now came into contact with a Russian family, whom he had known in St. Petersburg, and who took him with them for a rest cure in Ischia.

But his health was completely disintegrated. A few more concerts in Vienna, and Field returned to Moscow—broken in health and spirit. In November of 1836, he was once again confined to his bed. On January 11, 1837, he died.

His principal compositions include seven concertos for piano and orchestra, many sonatas for the piano, the nocturnes, a piano quintet and miscellaneous pieces. This is not a prolific output, but—to judge from those works of Field which I have had an opportunity to study—maintains a high level of artistic excellence. Field always possessed a good feeling for form, a vein of poetry which he could express in melodies of unforgettable beauty, good taste, refinement, and feeling. Had he avoided the temptations that accompanied wealth and a soft life and devoted himself to a life of disciplined creativeness, he might have grown and developed into an immortal; certainly the seeds of genius are fertilized in all his works. As it is, he is a composer of pages of beautiful music which should not be neglected. One might hesitate to say with Rellstab and Blom that Field's nocturnes are superior to Chopin's; yet one cannot deny—after an intimate acquaintance with them—that they deserve a place beside them. When will the world of music turn to Field and rediscover a wealth of beauty which, for so long a time, it has left virtually untouched?

§ 2

THE waltz has found its greatest composers in the second Johann Strauss, in Brahms, in Chopin, in Richard Strauss. But its great pioneer was a young blond-haired Viennese composer, Josef Lanner. Favorite of the café for two decades, Josef Lanner ushered in the era of Viennese light music which was brought to such magnificent culmination by Johann Strauss, father and son. Yet this was not his outstanding achievement. We are today inclined to consider Lanner merely as a brilliant personality in a period heralding the dawn of Vienna's heyday as the city of wine and song. But he was certainly much more than just an appealing Kapellmeister of the Viennese café.

For one thing, Lanner was himself a composer of many charming waltzes. It is quite true that he is not, even at his best, a composer of the artistic stature of the younger Johann Strauss; in the entire output of Lanner's maturest period there does not appear, I am sure, a waltz comparable to the *Tales from the Vienna Woods,* or the *Artist's Life,* or the *Vienna Blood.* And though he was one of the first to bring artistic dignity and prestige to a formerly despised dance form, he never quite translated this dance form into music of such transcendent quality as did Chopin or Brahms. For Josef Lanner was fated to inaugurate an era, not to bring it to its final fruition. Yet, I feel convinced, musical history can boast of few figures like Lanner, who succeeded not only in pointing out a new road, but also in traveling a considerable distance upon it himself.

If Lanner, at his best, never achieved such high inspiration as Chopin or Brahms or the younger Johann Strauss, his works, at any rate, persistently suggest the peaks towards which serious waltz writing might reach in the hands of a greater creative talent. There are, it seems to me, more moments of pure enchantment in the best waltzes of Lanner than in the waltzes of any other composer of Viennese light music with the exception of the younger Johann Strauss—who must remain incomparable in his field. And, certainly, the Strausses not only learned a valuable technical lesson from Lanner but also drew inspiration from his high moments of beauty. For like the younger Strauss, Lanner had the gift of spontaneity and freshness. If waltzes like the *Schönbrunnerwalzer* and the *Romantikerwalzer* did not have that wonderful integration of form and aptness of musical phrase of, say, the *Wine, Woman and Waltz,* they had, to a great extent, something of the Strauss pulse and movement, the frequent poignancy of utterance and that richness of melodic invention. They were, like the Strauss waltzes, symphonies of the dance—utilizing the fullest resources of thematic development, of harmony, of rhythm, of counterpoint. The *Abendsternwalzer* and the *Hoffnungswalzer,* too, are at their best not of the artistic stature of Strauss at his greatest; but they are characterized by that supple ability to give expression to pleasure and pain with alternate strokes of the pen, to sketch a melodic line that is nimble-footed, to enlarge an original theme into an imaginative development of a complex texture (a capacity which one does not usually associate with a composer of light music), and, finally, to produce a vitality which to this day has lost little of its zest, thrust, magnetic attraction. What if Lanner occasionally descends to a cheap phrase or a formalistic melody? What if he did not possess to a high degree a sense for self-criticism? The qualities that brought the great Johann Strauss waltzes their immortality can frequently be found in Josef Lanner. It is a sorry mistake to exclude him from the ranks of the great waltz composers of all time.

But Josef Lanner's importance in musical history rests not with his significance as a creator but with his contributions as a pioneer, as an influence. He was one of the greatest single forces in the artistic development of the waltz form. It is no exaggerated enthusiasm to say that the brilliant waltzes of the Johann Strauss family were largely made possible because he preceded them. A comparison of a waltz by Lanner with one of his distinguished forerunners—Mozart or Beethoven or Schubert—brings us the recognition of the amazing transformation that the waltz achieved with Lanner's works. With Mozart, Beethoven, and Schubert the melodic material of the waltz may frequently be richer in variety and imagination and less likely to assume the outlines of a cliché; also, the rhythmic and harmonic vocabulary is more varied and ingenious. But in comparison with a Lanner waltz, the waltzes of these great composers are inchoate in structure. The Schubert waltzes, moreover, appealed to the intellect; those of Lanner, to the feet.

From the germs of the waltz—as found in those early

dances such as the German *Teutsche* or more especially the Viennese *Ländler*—to the waltz of Franz
Schubert (and it must be remembered that Schubert
and Lanner were contemporaries) is no great step in
the evolution of the form. The earliest dance forms
were binary: for the most part two sections consisting
of eight-bar sentences.

The milestones in the development of the Viennese
waltz are not many; and they mark the road straight
to Josef Lanner. In Vienna, the *Ländler* and *Teutsche*
—dances which elsewhere were generally slow and slug-
gish, since they were danced by heavy peasant feet—
grew faster in tempo and lighter in spirit. The polished
dance floors of the Viennese palaces and the graceful
sandals of the Viennese nobility made for nimbleness
of foot. In November of 1786 what is generally considered the first true Viennese waltz took the city by
storm. It was the closing number of the second act to
an opera by Vicente Martín y Solar, *Una cosa rara*.[1]
Thereafter the popularity of the waltz grew in Vienna.
It passed from the nobility to the masses, who, having
found the dance, now held to it. Ruthlessly oppressed

---

[1] It is well known how amusingly Mozart quoted an air from
this opera in *Don Giovanni*. It might also be mentioned that
Haydn wrote an aria for *Una cosa rara*.

by a tyrannical government and an omnipresent police, the people found escape in waltzing. It was computed that every fourth person in Vienna could be found at one time or another in a ballroom. At the Carnival balls at the Redoutensaal, it was the waltz that met with the greatest demand and favor. As a friend of Mozart, Michael Kelly, remarked in his memoirs: "I thought waltzing from ten at night until seven in the morning a continual whirligig, and most tiring to the eye and ear."

In my time, the people in Vienna had the dance mania. When carnival time drew near, merriment broke out everywhere; with the advent of the festival period proper its manifestations exceeded all bounds. . . . The passion for dancing and masquerades was so pronounced among the Viennese ladies that nothing could make them curtail their favorite amusement. This went so far that for expectant mothers who could not be induced to stay at home separate rooms were provided with all conveniences; rooms indeed in which the child could be brought into the world if unhappily this should prove necessary.

And this was as early as 1786!

Viennese hearts being light (the censorship and oppression notwithstanding!) and morality in Vienna being lower than elsewhere in Europe, the waltz acquired greater and greater abandon. The waltz of *Una cosa rara* (marked *andante con moto*) was sedate and dignified in comparison to *Ach du lieber Augustin!* to which Vienna danced lustily towards the close of the century. Indeed, the rest of Europe was shocked by the indecencies of the Viennese waltz. Wrote the poet, Ernst Moritz Arndt, after witnessing a waltz for the first time:

> The dancers held up the dresses of their partners very high, wrapped themselves lightly in this shroud, bringing both bodies under one covering, as close together as possible, and thus the turning went on in the most indecent positions; the hand holding the dress lay hard against the breasts, pressing lasciviously at every moment; the girls, meanwhile, looked half insane and ready to swoon.

In many countries in Europe the dancing of the waltz was prohibited by law. As late as 1825 the waltz was defined in a European handbook of terms as "the name of a riotous and obscene German dance."

But in Vienna the waltz thrived. The German composer, Reichardt, who visited Vienna in 1809 wrote
that "the love of dancing is now intensified here to the
point of becoming a dance mania." And this dance
mania found its greatest satisfaction in waltzing. "How
potent is the attraction exercised by the waltz," remarked Count de la Garde upon seeing it danced in
Vienna. "As soon as the first bars start, countenances
are cleared, eyes sparkle and bodies are attacked by
anticipatory tremors. . . . Finally, ecstatic delight
breathed from charming faces when fatigue forced their
owners to leave the heavenly regions and gather new
strength from the earth."

It was Hummel who is believed to have been the
first composer to suggest the artistic possibilities of the
waltz by combining several waltzes into one and adding to them a *coda* as a sort of summation. In 1810,
Hummel composed a set of ten waltzes for the opening of the luxurious and slightly disreputable Apol-
losaal in Vienna. This was the first of the concert
waltzes. During the summer of 1819, Karl Maria von
Weber composed in Dresden the *Invitation to the
Waltz,* another successful example of the enlarged waltz
form. But, as Hanslick pointed out, until Lanner, the
waltz was hardly more than a *schwitzender Stubentanz*

("a sweaty and humdrum dance"). It was for Lanner to bring to it the refinement and grace and suppleness which have since become the identifying characteristics of every great waltz, whether Austrian, German or French.

A Lanner waltz continued in the direction pointed out by Hummel and Weber. A Lanner waltz consisted of an introduction (which foreshadowed the theme of the principal waltz). There followed a series of different waltzes, in which one principal waltz asserted itself prominently again and again within the texture. These waltzes were etched with a subtle variety of colors and shades, with a wide range of emotional expression which passed from light-footed gaiety to a pain that stabbed the heart. The entire series of waltzes was, finally, brought to a close with a well-knit coda which was often a summation of all the major waltz themes. It will, therefore, be seen that Johann Strauss inherited his form almost in its entirety from Lanner.

With the Congress of Vienna the popularity of the waltz assumed Gargantuan proportions. Almost everybody danced—and when they danced it was to the intoxicating strains of waltz-music. It was on the crest of this wave of popularity for the waltz that Josef Lanner was swept to fame.

Josef Lanner, the son of a Viennese glovemaker, was born on April 12, 1801, in the St. Ulrich district of Vienna, now the lower part of the eighth district below the Ringstrasse. In 1801 Vienna was already the musical center of Europe. Mozart had been dead only ten years and, though he had died in obscurity, his last opera, *Die Zauberflöte,* was already a great success at Schikaneder's theatre, Auf-der-Wieden. Haydn, living a quiet old age, was creating his last great works. Beethoven had signaled the passing of his apprenticeship with a monumental concert, held one year earlier, which introduced his first symphony and his first piano concerto to Viennese music lovers. Franz Schubert was four years old, already showing unmistakable signs of precociousness.

Lanner, too, was precocious. Almost from the first his talent reached for the popular rather than the serious in music. He was only twelve years old when Michael Pamer—he who composed some of Vienna's most robust dance melodies—asked him to join his band as violinist. For a while, Lanner worked with Pamer, but, finally, repelled by his employer's mode of living, deserted the band. For a period, his only connection with music was the chamber concerts he organized with the aid of a few friends at his father's house.

But his burning ambition was to have an orchestra of his own, like Pamer, and to direct it in the café music so loved by the Viennese. In 1819 he brought his ambition to modest realization. Together with his friends, the Dahanek brothers—one a guitarist, the other a violinist—he formed a trio which would stroll in the evenings through the Prater making music and calling for donations. On Sunday evenings, they would play in a café garden in the Leopoldstadt district, a favorite rendezvous for young blood.

Lanner's success was rapidly achieved. From Pamer he had learned several important lessons in performing popular music—such as the discreet use of rubatos —and to these he added his own taste and intuition. Besides, this fair-haired, blue-eyed, and slender young musician had what Pamer lacked: an appealing presence, a personality that could charm and delight as much as the music. The Lanner trio, therefore, soon became a favorite in the Leopoldstadt. Then other cafés called for its haunting music. At the *Grünen Jäger,* the *Wallischen Bierhaus* in the Prater and, most important of all, at the famous *Goldenen Rebbuhn* in the Goldschmiedgasse, Lanner became the reigning favorite of the Viennese.

One day, late in 1819, the younger Dahanek introduced Lanner to a young violist, then fifteen years old, who, he thought, might become a useful addition to the small ensemble. His name was Johann Strauss. Actually, Lanner had met this young Strauss some years earlier when together they played in Pamer's band; but it was now that he first came to know the younger man well.

The younger man was later to become the father of the composer of *The Blue Danube* and a waltz king in his own right. Thus, the paths of the first two great waltz composers in Vienna's history—Lanner and the first Strauss—crossed and joined.

With Johann Strauss' early history, Lanner was well acquainted. Johann was three years younger than Lanner. He was born on March 14, 1804, in the little beer shop, *Zum Guten Hirten*. There, as a child, Strauss came frequently into contact with German and Austrian dance music—those sprightly *Teutsche* and *Ländler* which were to be the source of his later waltzes. Musicians from Linz frequently disembarked near the *Hirten* from the Danube ships, and put up for the night at the inn where they would entertain the guests with dance tunes. Strauss, as a child, absorbed dance music; like Lanner he dreamed of the time when he would become a café-house musician.

Business reverses had driven Strauss' father to suicide when Johann was only one year old. After Strauss' mother remarried, Johann's stepfather apprenticed him to a bookbinder. Bookbinding was work which Johann detested. He much preferred his violin, which he had received as a gift while he was still a child, and from which he was almost inseparable. Finally, Johann decided to escape from a destiny which seemed intent on making him a craftsman. He ran away one night, wandering first through the streets of the city, then to the outskirts. A kindly fate soon brought him back to music. A violinist who had frequently visited the *Hirten* found him, adopted him, and gave him lessons on the violin. It was not long before Strauss could play the violin well enough to join the famous band of Michael Pamer.

Such was Strauss' history before his life became inextricably intertwined with that of Lanner. Actually, Strauss' history begins with his friendship with Lanner, for it was with Lanner that Strauss developed as a musician and enriched his personality.

Lanner took to young Strauss. They were both made of the same cloth. Both were easy-going, lovable, full of spirit and enthusiasm. They wore that charming

[225]

Viennese devil-may-care air. They both believed in the same Bohemian *Weltanschauung* which called for living today and letting tomorrow go hang. They shared a room in the *Windmühle* and lived a gay life in which they shared each other's pleasures, responsibilities, clothing, and debts. They were the town's most notorious pranksters.

They were also musical partners in the café. As Lanner's star continued to rise in the foremost café-houses, its satellite proved to be young Strauss. From Lanner, Strauss learned how to cut a figure of grace and charm when, with violin in hand, he directed his musicians in popular tunes performed with fetching appeal— with tender caresses, sentimental retards, sharp contrasts of mood and pace. But even more than this Strauss learned from Lanner how to write dance music imaginatively. For his performances in the café-houses, Lanner wrote an abundant amount of new popular tunes, tunes which Strauss helped to perform and which he assimilated before he began to write melodies of his own.

Lanner was already giving dimensions to the new waltz. At first composing only Ländler, he was soon inspired by Weber's *Invitation to the Waltz* to paint on a larger canvas. Opus 7 was Lanner's first excursion in waltz music—and somewhat appropriately (as if to express his indebtedness) it included a few bars from the Weber masterpiece. But after that Lanner was to speak entirely for himself. The *Terpischorewalzer* which succeeded the earlier charming and infectious *Dornbacherländler* was one of Lanner's first successful realizations of an enlarged waltz form in which a variety of different waltzes, dominated by a leading waltz, are given artistic coherence through the use of an introduction and a concluding coda. After that, Lanner wrote abundantly. One waltz after another poured from him in an untiring creative flow. Sentimental waltzes—hundreds of them—with melodies as soft and feminine in texture as the personality of their composer.

Lanner's friend and musical associate, Johann Strauss, was not slow to imitate. If Lanner composed waltzes, well, Strauss, too, would compose them. Strauss' Opus 1, the *Täuberlwalzer* emerges from the Lanner matrix. Eventually, the elder Johann Strauss was to achieve a personality of his own in his waltzes. Masterpieces like his *Strains of the Lorelei and the Rhine,* and the *Red, Black and Gold* do not follow the strict structural pattern to which Lanner was ever a slave, but have an elasticity which permit the elder Strauss a wider gamut of artistic expression. But what Strauss

[227]

knew of the waltz, he learned from Lanner, and without his intimate association with Lanner's music he could not have written as he did.

Envy was soon destined to bring the artistic partnership of Lanner and Strauss to its end. Lanner's fame grew prodigiously. He became the beloved of the café, and his music sent all of Vienna dancing. So great was the demand for his music that he was compelled to have two orchestras playing simultaneously: one of them was directed by Lanner himself at the *Rebbuhn* while the other one was conducted by his best friend, Strauss, at the *Wallischen Bierhaus.*

But Johann Strauss was not altogether capable of accepting the growing success of his friend without bitterness. He felt that he, himself, conducted the popular music of the café-house no less charmingly nor less intoxicatingly than Lanner. Yet *his* orchestra was known as a Lanner orchestra; and even the waltz he had just composed, the *Täuberlwalzer,* was believed to have been composed by Lanner. Johann Strauss was not the one to enjoy reflected glory. He starved for recognition for himself; and he dreamed of the time he could deflect the admiration of the Viennese towards his own name and music.

One evening at the Bock café, Johann Strauss announced to Lanner that he would set out on his own and start his own orchestra; the two friends almost came to blows. The rupture brought their musical partnership to a permanent end. Appropriately enough, Lanner spoke his sadness at this separation from a bosom friend in a waltz, *Trennungswalzer*.

The elder Johann Strauss made his début as Kapellmeister at the Bock café, and began a career which was to bring him to the heights. By 1830, he was conducting an orchestra of two hundred at the magnificent Sperl Redoutensaal. A bitter rivalry took place between Lanner's orchestra and Strauss', between Lanner's music and that of Strauss. Each had his faithful adherents. Each was to know the adulation of the Viennese caféhouses. Each was to become Kapellmeister of the Bürger regiment—one of the highest honors that a conductor of light music could achieve in Austria. But Strauss was soon to travel beyond Lanner. He was soon to know a fame which was not to be restricted by the boundaries of Vienna. In 1833, he began a series of tours throughout all of Europe which made his name as much a household word in leading European capitals as it was in Vienna.

This rivalry between Lanner and Strauss in Vienna

inevitably resulted in a growth of popularity for light music. And in this rivalry, the waltz—for both Lanner and Strauss composed abundantly, each attempting to outdo the latest success of his competitor—achieved its full stature as a musical form.

Josef Lanner died on August 14, 1843; the elder Johann Strauss followed him to the grave six years later. Their work was done. They had brought the waltz to its position of first importance in the social life of the Viennese. They had created a musical form, supple and resilient, which now awaited the hands of a master.

One year after Lanner's death, on October 15, 1844, the son of Johann Strauss (he, too, was called Johann Strauss) made his début as Kapellmeister and composer at the Dommayer Casino in Hietzing. The young Johann was a sensation. Nineteen times was he compelled to repeat his *Sinngedichtewalzer!* "Ah, these Viennese!" wrote Herr Wiest, editor of the *Wanderer*. "Exactly as they were ten years ago. A new waltz player —a piece of world history!" Then prophetically, Wiest added: "Good night, Lanner! Good evening, Father Strauss! Good morning, Son Strauss!"

Father Strauss did not live to hear *The Blue Danube* or the *Tales from the Vienna Woods* or the other fabrics of the waltz which the son was to weave so magically out of tones. But Father Strauss lived long enough to know that he had been eclipsed by his own son. His friend, Hirsch, had come to Dommayer's Casino to create a disturbance (for Father Strauss objected to a musical career for his estranged son); but he remained to cheer. And late that night he returned to the home of Father Strauss, who was lying sick in bed, to tell him that a new and greater waltz king had arisen.

IF MUSICAL history today treats Franz Liszt with the veneration it accords to its greatest masters, it is not because Liszt was essentially a great composer. He was an *important* composer, rather than a *great* one. His music—however great its artistic shortcomings may be—has influenced the direction of musical history and has helped to shape its destiny. As the father of the symphonic poem, a form which the modern composer has found so adaptable for his orchestral writing, Liszt stands with the great pioneers in music. Cecil Gray speaks of him as the "most important germinative force in modern music," while Philip Hale has written that "the more recent Germans and even the modern French were made possible by this Hungarian." He influenced others to write great music, even though he never composed great music himself.

For, as a composer, he was at best in the ranks of those lesser creators who had talent without genius, who had technique without the important ideas or concepts which such a technique can serve, who had the imagination to dream heroic dreams without that spark of genius which brings these dreams to successful realization on paper. Skill, resourcefulness, intelligence, scholarship—these he brought to his composing; but that additional quality, which can transform skill and scholarship into music of warmth, pulse and heart-beat, was rarely his. His music is not of the stuff of which masterpieces are made. It has moments of high flights, but these are too frequently separated by pages that are trite and obvious.

He conceived great tonal structures (just as Bruckner did) and hoped to fill them with conceptions of epical scope. But with Liszt, even more than with Bruckner, what left the hand was not a mighty epic, but rather ambitious yet unrealized pretensions, insincere postures. Beethoven might have made of Liszt's *Faust* and *Dante* symphonies works not only heroic in the proportions of their structure, but equally heroic in the depth of their ideas and in the quality of their speech. With Liszt, these works, Gargantuan though they are in outline, are more often bombastic than profound, more often sentimental than poignant in emotion, more often pompous than dramatic.

A composer's music is as his personality. If he lacks

integration as a man it is hardly likely that he will achieve it as an artist. Franz Liszt, the man, had many qualities, and many of them were so contradictory to each other that it has always been a difficult task for his biographers to draw a clear portrait of him. He was, for example, a blending of both the religious and the worldly. Religion dominated his life long before he embraced the Catholic Church as an Abbé. Yet, at the same time, he was more of the flesh than the spirit. He was a lover of women (one biographer has recorded the fact that Liszt had more than twenty-five love affairs!), of soft living, of luxury, pomp and ceremony. At certain times he was humble and self-effacing; at others, he was a super-egotist who demanded flattery and attention. He could live the life of a recluse and yet, on other occasions, could incessantly demand the society of sycophantic admirers and the fawning company of the high-born.

Which was the *real* Liszt? The spiritual or the worldly? The humble or the egotist? The recluse or the habitué of the Parisian salon?

He could be a severe and exacting artist of unscrupulous integrity; and yet he wrote potboilers. He could be generous to a fault (his charitable acts to causes or fellow-artists in need were famous), and yet at other

[*234*]

times he was hard, severe, even callous. He could be simple and warm-hearted, and he could be snobbish and hypocritical.

The true Liszt, stripped of postures, pretenses and poses, has eluded his biographers. And the *real* Liszt, as composer, has evaded his critics. As the man, so the composer. He lacked a clearly defined personality. He was many things, some of them contradicting each other; consequently, he was nothing. In all the abundance produced by his tireless pen there are no qualities which we can point to as unmistakably belonging to Liszt, just as there are qualities which we can analyze as incontrovertibly those of Bach or Beethoven or Brahms or Wagner in the works of these four masters. Sometimes in his music he was of the heart, other times of the head; sometimes he was sensuous, at other times, spiritual. Not only in different works, but often in one and the same work (as in the *Faust* symphony) he strove for the rhapsodic, epic, lyric, pensive. He combined a love for the theatrical with a frequent striving for simplicity. A sickly sentimentality often struggles in his music with intellectual pronouncements. A sensual lyricism is often combined with spiritual counterpoint. He never seemed to know in which element he was truly himself. He never learned which

[235]

style best represented his personality—whether the religious and often grandiose utterances of his oratorios, whether the gypsy hot-blood of his rhapsodies, whether the treacle of his *Liebestraum,* whether the soft, old-fashioned sentiments of his piano concertos, whether the cerebral pretensions of his symphonies, whether the theatricalism of his symphonic-poems, the *Todtentanz* or the *Mephisto* waltz, whether the superficial glitter and sparkle of many of his pieces for the piano and the *Fantasia on the Ruins of Athens,* whether the solid musicianship of his transcriptions for the piano. . . .

It is not an accident that the only works of Liszt to have retained their popularity with music audiences are those which are least pretentious, those works which are pleasant, dramatically effective, lyrical and singularly unimportant, such as the two piano concertos, the piano sonata, the *Liebestraum,* the Hungarian Rhapsodies, and the symphonic poem, *Les Préludes.* For Liszt was essentially a maker of theatrical music, music to warm the blood and arouse the senses; sublimity, spirituality, profundity—these were for greater composers than he. Edward Dannreuther accurately gauged Liszt's artistic shortcomings when he wrote in the *Oxford History of Music:*

In place of melody, Liszt offers mere fragments of melody—touching, it may be, and
beautiful, passionate or tinged with triviality; in
lieu of a rational distribution of centers of harmony in accordance with some definite plan, he
presents clever combinations of chords and ingenious modulations from point to point; in lieu
of musical logic and consistency of design, he is
content with rhapsodical improvisation. The
power of persistence seems wanting, orchestral
polyphony is not attempted. The musical growth
is spoilt, the development of the themes is
stopped or perverted by some reference to ex-
traneous ideas. Everywhere the programme
stands ·in the way and the materials refuse to
coalesce.

·It is not impossible that Liszt's almost schoolboy-
ish adoration of Wagner arose from his conscious realization that the composer of *Tristan und Isolde* possessed what he, with all his skill and erudition, lacked:
greatness of spirit, greatness of thought, greatness of
feeling.

But as a pioneer he is of the rank of Wagner. Liszt's
ideas were always greater than their realization. He

groped for a new symphonic form that was more completely unified, more of one piece, than the symphony
—one movement in place of four, and that movement
unrestricted by the definitely marked out barriers of
the sonata form. He conceived such a symphonic form
as the translator into tones of poetry, or a dramatic
text, or the message of a painting, or an idea, or a definite story. To give such a text greater musical articulateness he borrowed the *idée fixe* from Berlioz (or the
Leitmotif as Wagner was to employ it). And—always
apt in his choice of names—he called his new symphonic form a "tone-poem" or "symphonic poem."

He composed twelve works in this new symphonic
form, and he came to them by way of his passion for
literature. He was about twenty-eight years old, when
—a magnificent career as virtuoso of piano behind him
—he was suddenly seized in Paris by a whim to abandon music. He came into personal contact with some
of the leading spirits in the French literature of the
time—Lamartine, Victor Hugo, George Sand—and was
strongly influenced by them. He turned to the reading
of philosophy and literature, devouring the works of
Montaigne, Chateaubriand, Voltaire, Sainte-Beuve, Lamartine, Rousseau, and others. "Monsieur Crimieux,"
he wrote to his friend, "please teach me *all* of French

[238]

literature." His obsession with literature and philosophy proved so great that he neglected himself—forgot to eat or sleep regularly. He suffered a nervous breakdown, and at one time was so sick that a rumor spread throughout all of Paris that he had died.

Momentarily, during the revolution of 1830, he deflected his passion for philosophy into politics. He was fired by the cause of the proletariat, and it was only with difficulty that his mother could prevent him from fighting on the barricades.

But he soon returned to music, and combined his voracious reading with his composition. At this time he wrote:

> Here is a whole fortnight that my mind and my fingers have been working like two spirits—Homer, the Bible, Locke, Byron, Hugo, Lamartine, Chateaubriand, Beethoven, Bach, Hummel, Mozart, Weber are all around me. I study them, meditate on them, devour them with fury. . . . Ah! provided I don't go mad, you will find an artist in me! Yes, an artist such as you desire, such as is required nowadays.

Inevitably, he tried to make oneness out of the dichotomy of literature and music. He knew Berlioz's

Symphonie fantastique well, admired it passionately
—had, as a matter of fact, made a piano transcription
of it the day after he had heard it for the first time.
Berlioz first revealed to him how music and literature
could serve each other, how in the hands of an imaginative composer music can become vividly programmatic. Having learned a method from Berlioz (even up
to the use of the *idée fixe* for unification), he now
groped for a form more flexible, terser than the symphony. He conceived a one-movement form in which
ideas are permitted to germinate freely at the will of
the composer, to grow and change unhampered by the
restrictions of any set architectonic structure. Such a
form, he felt could become a musical poem in the hands
of a true musical poet. . . .

Thus, after 1830, Liszt began to draw more and
more from literature for programmatic material for
his tone-poems. He drew inspiration from Goethe, from
Victor Hugo, from Shakespeare, from Lamartine, from
Schiller—and this material became the programmatic
source for his music.

Like Richard Strauss after him, Liszt leaned heavily
on a literary program. In his tone-poems he attempted
to build up a character, depict dramatic episodes, or
suggest some literary thesis. His *Tasso,* for example,

was a portrait of a hero; it was Liszt's *Heldenleben.*
It was, as Liszt himself explained, an attempt to speak
musically about

> the genius who was misjudged during his life;
> surrounded after death with a halo that de-
> stroyed his enemies. Tasso loved and suffered at
> Ferrara; he was avenged at Rome; his glory still
> lives in the folk-songs of Venice. These three ele-
> ments are inseparable from his immortal mem-
> ory. To represent them in music, I first called
> up his august spirit as he still haunts the waters
> of Venice. Then I beheld his proud and melan-
> choly figure as he passed through the festivals
> of Ferrara where he had produced his master-
> pieces. Finally I followed him to Rome, the eter-
> nal city, that offered him the crown and glorified
> in him the martyr and the poet.

Les Préludes, the most famous of his tone-poems, is
another musical translation of a definite program, this
time a rather metaphysical text by Lamartine. *Mazeppa,* inspired by a poem of Victor Hugo, is a literal
musical translation of the sufferings of the famous
Asiatic chieftain during a historic ride in which, for
three days, he gallops on a fiery steed over plains and

hills. Finally, the horse succumbs to fatigue. The tone-poem ends with a description of the birds that fly over horse and hero.

Tasso, Les Préludes, and *Mazeppa* are the only three of Liszt's tone-poems which have survived. They are, for the most part, as second rate in their musical inspiration as other of Liszt's works. Too often, as in *Les Préludes,* Liszt's music acquires almost stock-company theatricalness. *Tasso,* in which Liszt reached for eloquence, is bombastic, while *Mazeppa* is almost naïve in its attempt to translate a set program into music literally. But even second-rate music can have historic significance. In these works, Liszt clearly defined a new form, and definitely established programmatic writing for the orchestra. Where he failed, others were to succeed. Two years after Liszt's death, a young German composer, Richard Strauss, was to compose the first of his immortal tone-poems.

Liszt was a pioneer in still another musical form which has played a significant part in the music of our times. Just as Richard Strauss was evolved from his tone-poems, so can we trace the source of important works by such composers as Brahms, Enesco, and even

George Gershwin to Liszt's famous Hungarian Rhapsodies.

In 1840, Franz Liszt returned to his native country and while there he was moved by the kinesthetic, rhythmic appeal and aroused by the hot blood of gypsy music. This gypsy music he yearned to perpetuate in a large musical form. Since he could find no structure adequate for his purpose, his resourcefulness once again evolved a new form which, like the tone-poem, gave the composer full freedom of expression. What he desired was a free fantasia form in which he could string together a variety of different folk tunes, with sharp contrasts of mood, rhythm and color. Thus he invented the rhapsody. The name of "rhapsody" he derived from the Greeks who called the ballads of their epic poets by that name; each book of Homer's *Iliad,* for example, was a "rhapsody." But with Liszt, the rhapsody became no mere ballad nor a part of an epic, but rather a form complete in itself, treated imaginatively and freely, in which the many melodies are given breathing space and *Lebensraum.* It may be, as Edward J. Dent points out, that Liszt found the prototype for his rhapsody in a work which he knew well and admired, the Schubert *Divertissement à la hongroise.* But, certainly, the Schubert work is no rhapsody as we know and recognize the form today. It was Liszt who discovered it, and Liszt who brought it to artistic importance. Whatever may be the artistic shortcomings of his Hungarian Rhapsodies (and though they have an emotional appeal it is hardly possible to accept them as important music), they are pioneers and as such deserve a gesture of recognition on the part of history. Out of them has sprung the music of the remarkable piano rhapsodies of Brahms (which, though they are not based on folk material, are nevertheless Lisztian in approach and scope) and orchestral compositions by modern composers everywhere, including Ravel (*Rapsodie espagnole*), Alfven (*Swedish Rhapsody*), Enesco (the Rumanian rhapsodies), and Sir Edward German (*A Welsh Rhapsody*).

APPENDICES

GUIDE TO RECORDED MUSIC

I. THE EARLY OPERA AND ORATORIO

I

PERI: *Euridice, "Funeste piagge."* Coupled with CAC-
CINI: *Euridice, "Non piango."* VICTOR 21752

MONTEVERDI: *Arianna,* "Lament." PARLAPHONE
R1024

Orfeo, "Ecco purch'a voi ritorno." VICTOR 21747
L'Incoronazione di Poppea, "Oblivion soave." CO-
LUMBIA DB500

CAVALLI: *Xerse,"Beato chu puo."* MIA 4

PURCELL: *Dido and Aeneas* (complete). DECCA AL-
BUM

RAMEAU: *Castor et Pollux,* "Tristes apprêts." COLUM-
BIA LF18

Ballet Music. BRUNSWICK 90316

II

CARISSIMI: *Ezechias,* Air of Ezechias. COLUMBIA DFX
43

A. SCARLATTI: Cantata, *"Io vi miro ancor."* VICTOR
7658

SCHÜTZ: *"Eile mich Gott zu erreten."* Coupled with

APPENDIX

"*O süsse, o freundlicher, o gütiger Herr.*" KANTOREI 5
Psalms 40, 51 and 111. ANTHOLOGIE SONORE 57

III

GLUCK: *Orfeo* (almost complete). COLUMBIA OPERA
SET 15
    Iphigénie en Aulide, Overture. COLUMBIA X1138
    —"*Diane impitoyable!*" Coupled with "*O toi l'objet
    le plus aimable.*" GRAMOPHONE E5490
    Iphigénie en Tauride, "*Unis dès la plus tendre en-
    fance.*" COLUMBIA 9116M
    —"*O malheureuse Iphigénie!*" DECCA LY6065
PICCINNI: *Didon,* Air of Didon. GRAMOPHONE K7342

IV

PERGOLESI: *La Serva Padrona,* Vocal Selections.
DECCA LY6014
ROUSSEAU: *Le Devin du Village,* Four Airs. ANTHO-
LOGIES SONORE 130

II. EARLY INSTRUMENTAL MUSIC

I

FRESCOBALDI: Fugue in G-minor. VICTOR 1663
    Toccata for the Elevation. ANTHOLOGIE SONORE 4
BUXTEHUDE: Two chorale preludes (coupled with
two chorale preludes of Pachelbel). MUSICRAFT 1050
    Fugue in F-major (coupled with chorale preludes
of Pachelbel). GRAMOPHONE FM23

[*248*]

Prelude and Fugue in E-major.   ARTIPHONE D12083
Prelude, Fugue and Chaconne.   ODEON 25496
Chorale prelude, *"Komm' Heiliger Geist"* (coupled
   with Pachelbel chorale preludes).   KANTOREI 16

II

CORELLI: Concerto grosso #12, "Christmas Concerto."
   VICTOR M600
   Sonata #12, *"La Folia."*   GRAMOPHONE DB1501
   Suite for String Orchestra.   COLUMBIA X52067
   Sonata da camera (Trio), B-flat major.   PRO MUSICA
   106

III

KUHNAU: "The Combat Between David and Goliath."
   ANTHOLOGIE SONORE 3
COUPERIN: Miscellaneous Harpsichord Works, Cou-
   perin Society Album.   HIS MASTER'S VOICE
D. SCARLATTI: Twenty Sonatas, Scarlatti Sonata So-
   ciety.   HIS MASTER'S VOICE
K. P. E. BACH: Sonata in G-Major.   MUSICRAFT 1012
   Sonata in A-minor.   VICTOR M606
   Sonata in F-minor, 1st movement.   COLUMBIA DB-
   830
   Sonata in G-major, 2nd movement.   COLUMBIA DB-
   831

IV

DITTERSDORF: Quartet in A-major.   MUSICRAFT M49

[*249*]

III. A FEW MUSICAL FORMS

I

FIELD: Nocturne in A-major. COLUMBIA DB1232

II

LANNER: *Schönbrunnerwalzer.* TELEFUNKEN E990

J. STRAUSS (father): *Donaulieder.* GRAMOPHONE C2338
  Strains of the Lorelei and the Rhine. POLYDOR
    22429
  Radetzky March. VICTOR 4127

III

LISZT: Hungarian rhapsody, Number 2. VICTOR 6652
  —Number 6. GRAMOPHONE B4284
  —Number 12. COLUMBIA C7243
  —Number 14. VICTOR 4187
  Les Préludes. VICTOR M453
  Mazeppa. PARLAPHONE R1579

BIBLIOGRAPHY

Adler, Guido, *Handbuch der Musikgeschichte*, Berlin, 1930

Ambros, A. W., *Geschichte der Musik*, Leipzig, 1909

Apthorp, W. F., *The Opera Past and Present*, New York, 1901

Bachmann, A., *Les grands violinistes du passé*, Paris, 1913

Bekker, Paul, *The Changing Opera*, New York, 1935

Bellaigue, C., *Études musicales* (2e série), Paris, 1903

———— *Musical Studies and Silhouettes*, New York, 1901

Berlioz, Hector, *Gluck and his Operas*, London, 1914

Blaze, François Henri (Castil-Blaze), *L'Opéra en France*, Paris, 1820

———— *Les Débuts de la musique en Venise*, Brussels, 1914

Bruyr, Jean, *Grétry*, Paris, 1931

Burney, Charles, *A General History of Music*, New York, 1935

Chantavoine, Jean, *De Couperin à Debussy*, Paris, 1921

Closson, Ernest, *André Modeste Grétry*, Turnhout, 1920

Combarieu, J., *Histoire de la musique*, Paris, 1919

Cooper, Martin, *Gluck*, New York, 1935

Cucuel, Georges, *La Pouplinière et la musique du chambre au 18e siècle*, Paris, 1913

Cummings, William, *Purcell*, London (no date)

Decsey, Ernst, *Johann Strauss*, Stuttgart-Berlin, 1922

BIBLIOGRAPHY

Dent, Edward J., *Alessandro Scarlatti*, London, 1905

Dittersdorf, Karl von, *The Autobiography of Karl von Dittersdorf*, London, 1896

Dupré, Henri, *Purcell*, New York, 1928

Einstein, Alfred, *Gluck*, London, 1936

——— *Heinrich Schütz*, Kassel, 1928

Flood, W. H. Grattan, *John Field of Dublin*, Dublin, 1920

Godard, Joseph, *The Rise and Development of Opera*, London, 1912

Gradenwitz, Peter, *Johann Stamitz*, Brünn, 1936

Grétry, André, *Mémoires*, Paris, 1797

Haas, R., *Gluck und Durazzo*, Zurich, 1925

——— *Wiener Musiker vor und um Beethoven*, Vienna, 1927

Henderson, W. J., *Some Forerunners of Italian Opera*, New York, 1911

Hervey, Arthur, *Franz Liszt and His Music*, London, 1911

Hogarth, George, *Memoirs of the Music Drama*, London, 1838

——— *Memoirs of the Opera in Italy, France, Germany and England*, London, 1851

——— *Musical History, Biography and Criticism*, London, 1838

Huneker, James Gibbons, *Franz Liszt*, New York, 1911

Jacob, Heinrich, *Johann Strauss: Father and Son*, New York, 1939

Jullien, Adolphe, *La cour et l'opéra sous Louis XIV*, Paris, 1878

Kelly, Michael, *Musical Reminiscences*, London, 1826

Kobald, Karl, *Johann Strauss*, Vienna, 1925

[252]

Kilburn, Nicholas, *The Story of Chamber Music,* London, 1932

Krebs, K., *Dittersdorfiana,* Berlin, 1900

Kretzschmar, Hermann, *Geschichte der Opera,* Leipzig, 1919

Landowska, Wanda, *The Music of the Past,* New York, 1924

Lange, Fritz, *Josef Lanner und Johann Strauss,* Leipzig, 1919

Laurencie, Lionel de la, *Les créateurs de l'opéra français,* Paris, 1930

———— *Rameau,* Paris, 1926

Lavoix, Henri, *Histoire de la musique française,* Paris, 1891

Mackinlay, Sterling, *The Origin and Development of Light Opera,* London, 1927

Marmontel, J. F., *Essai sur les révolutions de la musique en France,* Paris, 1777

Marx, A. B., *Gluck und die Opera,* Berlin, 1863

Masson, P. M., *L'Opéra de Rameau,* Paris, 1930

Moser, Hans J., *Heinrich Schütz: Sein Leben und Werke,* Kassel, 1936

Nef, Karl, *An Outline of the History of Music,* New York, 1935

Oxford History of Music, vol. 3, *The Music of the Seventeenth Century* by C. Hubert Parry, London, 1902
vol. 6, *The Romantic Period* by Edward Dannreuther, London, 1905

Parry, Charles Hubert, *The Evolution of the Art of Music,* New York, 1930

Pincherle, Marc, *Corelli,* Paris, 1933

———— *Feuillets d'histoire du violon,* Paris, 1927

[253]

BIBLIOGRAPHY

Pirro, André, *Dietrich Buxtehude*, Paris, 1913

—— *Heinrich Schütz*, Paris, 1913

Pougin, Arthur, *Monsigny et son temps*, Paris, 1908

Prunières, Henri, *Cavalli et l'opéra vénitien au 17e siècle*, Paris, 1931

—— *Claudio Monteverdi*, New York, 1926

Reuchsel, Maurice, *L'école classique du violon*, Paris, 1906

Riemann, H., *Handbuch der Musikgeschichte*, Leipzig, 1904–1913

Rolland, Romain, *A Musical Tour Through the Land of the Past*, London, 1922

—— *Les origines du théâtre lyrique moderne*, Paris, 1931

—— *Some Musicians of Former Days*, New York, 1915

Rousseau, J. J., *Écrits sur la musique*, Paris, 1838

Schering, Arnold, *Geschichte der Instrumental-Konzert*, Leipzig, 1927

—— *Geschichte des Oratoriums*, Leipzig, 1911

Schneider, Louis, *Un précurseur de la musique italienne au 16e et 17e siècle*, Paris, 1921

Seiffert, Max, *Geschichte der Klaviermusik*, Leipzig, 1899

Sitwell, Sacheverell, *A Background for Domenico Scarlatti*, London, 1935

Stahl, Wilhelm, *Buxtehude*, Kassel, 1937

Straeten, Edmund Joseph van der, *The History of the Violin*, London, 1931

Streatfeild, R. A., *The Opera*, London (no date)

Tessier, André, *Couperin*, Paris, 1926

Tiersot, Jullien, *Les Couperins*, Paris, 1926

BIBLIOGRAPHY

Blom, Eric, "John Field," *Chesterian,* vol. 11, p. 203, 1930

Bruyr, Jean, *"La Jeunesse de Grétry,"* La Revue musicale, vol. 12, p. 417, 1931

Calvocoressi, M. D., *"Un prédecesseur de Bach: Johann Kuhnau,"* Le Guide musicale, vol. 50, p. 43, 1904

Carse, Adam, "Monteverdi and His Orchestra," *Sackbut,* vol. 2, p. 12, 1921

Chrysander, Fr., "Couperin," *Monthly Musical Record,* vol. 19, p. 25, 1889

Dent, Edward J., "The Operas of Scarlatti," *Sammelbände der Internationalen Musik-Gesellschaft,* Sessions 42, p. 51, 1915–16

Erckmann, Fr., "Heinrich Schütz, *Monthly Musical Record,* vol. 52, p. 309, 1922

"Gluck-Heft," Die Musik, vol. 13, 1914

Hawkins, John, "The Life of Corelli," *Universal Magazine,* vol. 60, p. 169, London, 1777

Keller, Hermann, *"Johann Kuhnaus Klavierwerke,"* Neue Musikzeitung (Stuttgart), vol. 43, p. 272, 1922

Kurth, Ernst, *"Die Jugendopern Glucks bis Orfeo,"* Studien zur Musikwissenschaft, vol. 1, p. 193, 1913

Lesur, Daniel, "Heinrich Schütz," *La Revue musicale,* vol. 19, p. 112, 1937

Marchal, Robert, "Giulio Caccini," *La Revue musicale,* vol. 6, p. 140, 1925

Masson, Paul Marie, *"Le centenaire de Pergolesi,"* Le Guide du concert, vol. 1, p. 149, 1911

——— *"Lullistes et ramistes,"* L'Année musicale, vol. 1, p. 187, 1911

[255]

BIBLIOGRAPHY

Montague, Nathan M., "Russian John Field," *Monthly Musical Record,* vol. 48, p. 32, 1918

Montillet, William, *"L'Œuvre d'orgue de Dietrich Buxtehude,"* *La Revue musicale,* vol. 18, p. 109, 1937

Naylor, E. W., "Some Characteristics of Heinrich Schütz," *Musical Association Proceedings,* Sessions 32, p. 23, 1905

Parry, Charles Hubert, "The Significance of Monteverdi," *Musical Association Proceedings,* Sessions 42, p. 51, 1915

Persyn, Jean, *"Corelli, l'homme et l'œuvre,"* *Le Monde Musicale,* vol. 37, p. 310, 1926

Rendall, E. D., "Some Notes on Purcell's Dramatic Music," *Music and Letters,* vol. 1, p. 135, 1920

Rigler, G., *"Die Kammermusik Dittersdorfs,"* *Studien zur Musikwissenschaft,* vol. 14, p. 179, 1927

Sondheimer, Robert, "Gluck in Paris," *Zeitschrift für Musikwissenschaft,* vol. 5, p. 165, 1922

Souper, F. O., "Dittersdorf; His Fame and Fall," *Monthly Musical Record,* vol. 59, p. 43, 1929

———"The Music of Dittersdorf," *Music and Letters,* vol. 11, p. 141, 1930

Squire, W. Barclay, "Purcell's *Dido and Aeneas,*" *Musical Times,* vol. 59, p. 379, 1931

Tiersot, Jullien, "Rameau," *Menestral,* vol. 93, p. 379, 1931

Welti, Heinrich, *"Gluck und Calsabigi,"* *Vierteljahrschrift für Musikwissenschaft,* vol. 7, p. 26, 1891

Woodham, Ronald, "Dietrich Buxtehude," *Musical Times,* vol. 78, p. 787, 1937

BIBLIOGRAPHY

Bach, K. P. E., *Klavier Sonaten,* edited by Baumgart, Breslau, 1863

Buxtehude, D., *Orgelkompositionen,* edited by Spitta, Leipzig, 1876

Caccini, G., *Euridice* (in *Publikation altere* . . . *Musikwerke,* vol. 9–10, Berlin, 1881)

Cavaliere, Emilio de, *La Rappresentazione dell' anima e del corpo,* Rome, 1912

Cavalli, Giulio, *Il Giasone* (in *Publikation altere* . . . . *Musikwerke,* vol. 12, Berlin, 1883)

Corelli, Arcangelo, *Les Œuvres de Corelli,* 2 volumes, London, 188–

Couperin, François, *Œuvres complets,* vols. 2–5 (*Pièces de clavecin*), Paris, 1932

Deldevez, E. *Fondation de l'opéra en France,* Paris, 1875

Denkmäler deutscher Tonkunst, Leipzig

    vol. 4, *Kuhnaus Klavierwerke,* 1901

    vol. 11, Buxtehude, *Instrumentalwerke,* 1903

    vol. 61–62, Telemann, *Tafelmusik,* 1923

Denkmäler der Tonkunst in Bayern, Leipzig

    vol. 6, Pachelbel, *Orgelkompositionen,* 1903

    vol. 15, *Mannheimer Symphoniker,* 1907

    vol. 27–28, *Mannheimer Kammermusik der 18 Jahrhunderts,* 1914–1915

Denkmäler der Tonkunst in Österreich, Vienna

    vol. 1, Fux, *Messen,* 1894

    vol. 2, Fux, *Motetten,* 1894

    vol. 19, Fux, *Instrumentalwerke,* 1902

    vol. 31, *Wiener Instrumentalmusik,* 1908

    vol. 34–35, Fux, *Costanza e Fortezza,* 1910

BIBLIOGRAPHY

vol. 39, *Wiener Instrumentalmusik,* Auswahl 2, 1912

vol. 42–44, Gassmann, *La Contessina,* 1914

vol. 44a, Gluck, *Orfeo ed Euridice,* 1914

vol. 56, *Wiener Tansmusik,* 1921

vol. 65, Lanner, *Ländler und Walzer,* 1926

vol. 75, Caldara, *Kammermusik für Gesang,* 1932

vol. 81, Dittersdorf, *Drei Sinfonien,* 1936

Dittersdorf, Karl von, *Ausgewählte Orchesterwerke,* Leipzig, 1899–1904

Field, John, *Nocturnes,* ed. by Franz Liszt, New York, 1902

Gluck, Christoph Willibald, *Alceste,* Leipzig, 186–

————— *Iphigénie en Aulide,* Berlin, 187–

————— *Iphigénie en Tauride,* Leipzig, 1927

Liszt, Franz, *Musikalische Werke,* Serie I, Abt I, Leipzig, 1907

Monteverdi, Claudio, *Die Klage der Ariadne,* Mainz, 1931

————— *Orfeo,* Augsburg, 1927

Pergolesi, Giovanni, *La Serva Padrona,* Leipzig, 1890

Peri, Giacopo, *Euridice* (in Luigi Torchi's *L'Arte musicale in Italia,* vol. 6, Milan, 1897)

Purcell, Henry, *Dido and Aeneas,* London, 1925

Rameau, Jean Philippe, *Castor et Pollux,* Paris, 1880

Scarlatti, Domenico, *Opere complete per clavicembalo,* edited by Alessandro Longo, Milan, 1906

Schütz, Heinrich, *Sämmtliche Werke,* Leipzig, 1885–1927, vols. 1, 5, 7, 10–11, 18

Stamitz, Johann, *Sinfonien,* edited by Carl Wagner, Heidelberg, 1935

Straube, Karl, *Alte Meister des Orgelspiels,* Leipzig, 1929

INDEX

INDEX

INDEX

[*271*]

INDEX

INDEX

[*278*]

INDEX